Practical SQL

Copyright 2011 David Perry

* * * * *

"All of the books in the world contain no more information than is broadcast as video in a single large American city in a single year. Not all bits have equal value."
Carl Sagan

* * * * *

Practical SQL
Copyright 2011 David Perry

* * * * *

Table of Contents

About the Author

My name is David Perry and for as long as I can remember, I've been tinkering with some form of tech or another. This book, in specific, I am dedicating to my father since, in more than a biological sense, none of this would be possible without him. Some of my earliest memories are of sitting with my dad at the family 286. At first it was the kind of stuff you'd expect a 6 or 7 year old child to be doing: mostly games, but eventually our time in front of the black-and-amber screen turned to more serious pursuits. I wish I could say what provoked the foray into programming, but I honestly have no recollection. What I do recall vividly is the 5¼ inch floppy labeled "GW-BASIC" sliding into drive B and a short time later a centipede-like pattern of text crawling down the screen: left to right, then right to left, descending one row at a time. In that one program I had been taught how to construct nested loops, handle arrays, do simple math, simple string manipulation and output data to the screen; Quite an ambitious lesson, but I soaked it up like a sponge and haven't stopped since.

With time I graduated to more advanced languages, got better hardware, better operating systems and started to tackle a wider variety of problems. Finally, I came of age and got my first real programming gig – I was a web developer during the tail end of the dot-com bubble. The hours were long, but so were the vacations, and the money was decent, but the lessons learned were hard. In the years prior I'd solved purely erudite problems through code. I knew at least five ways to generate prime numbers and could rank their efficiency by scenario. I had tinkered with edge-finding algorithms, solved the Towers of Hanoi problem recursively and even played with the toughest of algorithms problems: the Traveling Salesman problem... And it was all useless. My customers didn't need that kind of skill, they needed an ASP script to pull information from a database. They needed CGI that could calculate shipping costs. They needed simple things, but skills that I had never acquired. Even after the bubble burst and my time in web design was over, these hard-learned lessons kept coming. Every class I took, every book I read, they were all filled with unrealistic lessons, often designed to teach concepts no one in the class was likely to ever use. The human brain can only store so much data, and it seemed like the traditional educational resources were intent on filling it with arbitrary useless junk. Something had to change.

Today, you can find a lot of answers on the internet, but these tend to be in two forms: very specific answers to very specific questions and extremely basic tutorials. The purpose I hope for this book to serve is to act as a "middle road" of sorts, more advanced than a tutorial, containing a fair selection of those "very specific answers" that I've come across the need for more than once; Complex enough to function as a textbook, but without the clutter. This is a book about SQL written by a Database Administrator and SQL Programmer specifically for those who might someday share my job title(s).

As it is the environment most of us will end up working in, the majority of this book will focus on Microsoft SQL Server and its associated tools, but there will be a small section at the end dedicated to the primary differences between Microsoft SQL Server and its most common competitor – especially in the small business market – MySQL.

* * * * *

Section 1: SQL Administration

Chapter 1: Introduction to Database Concepts

In nearly every aspect of our lives today, we generate information. Every trip to the grocery store likely involves a "club card" which tracks our purchasing habits. Even without such a card, the transaction itself as well as the inventory of every cantaloupe or box of crackers is also stored, updated and validated. It is nearly impossible to perform any action in modern society and NOT generate a record in a database somewhere, so it behooves us to have at least a basic comprehension of how that data is stored and what we can do with it.

The simplest definition of "database" is a collection of related information. We might imagine the real-world counterpart to the database as a file cabinet, able to hold many disparate bits of information, but all related to a common theme or process. Of course, the items in a file cabinet need not be related as a rule – I have a filing cabinet at my desk which holds files, tea and (most days) my lunch – but typically, file cabinets hold files full of documents, so our general definition holds.

In the beginning, databases were not as similar to file cabinets as our comparison might let on. The first databases had far less ability to sort and distribute information. These were the "flat file" databases of old. A "flat file" database places all of its data into individual files, which cannot be linked to one another in any way. If you have one file containing your customers' account numbers and names and another file containing their account numbers and outstanding balances, there is no way to produce a report containing their names and account balances – the data in each file stands alone. The limitations of such a system are immediately apparent: In order to always have the data you need, you have to store the same data in many places.

Realizing the inefficiencies of "flat file" databases, a mathematician working for IBM developed a model for what he called a "relational" database in the early 1970's. The model caught on and today almost all databases are relational. In relational databases, our two chunks of customer information can now be linked together in interesting ways. If our previous example had been a relational database, we could simply run a report saying "give me all of the account numbers and balances from the 2nd table and then use the account number to look up their name from the 1st table." This is both the benefit and detriment of relational databases: They add complexity, but in that complexity lies great power.

Regardless of what kind of database you use or what you use it for, there is some terminology that is absolutely necessary to understand database basics.

	A	B	C
1	Name	Account #	Balance
2	John Smith	123456	$100.00
3	Frank Jones	234567	$ 50.00
4	Jim White	345678	$150.00

Figure 1.1: Table, column, row, field

The above is actually a screenshot from a spreadsheet, a distant cousin of the database, but it serves as a good explanation of a few simple concepts. What we have is a collection of related data in a layout we call a "table." A table is composed of rows, columns and, in the case of a real database,

6

fields. In figure 1.1 the horizontal sets of data identified by numbers are rows, while the vertical sets identified by letters are columns. The bit where spreadsheets first begin to differ from databases is illustrated by the contents of row 1: Databases don't have "headers." Every row in a database table contains only data, but unlike a spreadsheet databases give us the ability to name those columns something more useful than A, B and C: We call these names "fields" and so a database would actually look more like this:

	Name	Account #	Balance
1	John Smith	123456	$ 100.00
2	Frank Jones	234567	$ 50.00
3	Jim White	345678	$ 150.00

Figure 1.2: That's more like it

Section 1.1: Joins

Now let's talk about the thing that makes relational databases powerful: Joins. Imagine you have the following two tables, we'll call them "Accounts" and "Balances."

Name	Account #	Account #	Balance
John Smith	123456	123456	$ 100.00
Frank Jones	234567	345678	$ 150.00

Figure 1.3: Accounts (left) and Balances (right)

In our previous example, we would have had no way to link these two tables of information together, but in a relational database our price paid in complexity has bought us that power in the form of a "join." A join is a statement that tells our database software to look for correlating data in two different tables and to show us a new (temporary) table containing that combined data. You might have noticed that Accounts and Balances both have some information missing. Account 234567 has a name, but no balance while account 345678 has a balance, but no name. What do we do in these (scarily common) circumstances? Well there are four different types of join operations we can perform:

- Left Join
  If we imagine our tables side by side, the left join specifies that the leftmost table is the most "important" and so all of its data will be displayed. Any data from the right-hand table which correlates to the left-hand table will also be displayed. Frank and John will be displayed, and John will have no balance.

- Right Join
  Again, imagining our tables side by side, this join specifies that the rightmost table is the most "important" and so all of its data will be displayed. Only data from the left-side table which correlates to the right-side table's data will be displayed. Account 123456 will be displayed, and show John's name, account 345678 will be displayed with no name and Frank (account 234567) will not be displayed at all.

- Inner Join
  The inner join is one of two "equal-opportunity" joins – an inner join will only show data which correlates across BOTH tables. In this case, it will show only the record for John, since his is the only account number that exists in both tables

- Outer Join
  Finally, the outer join is our other "equal opportunity" join. The outer join shows all data from both tables regardless of correlation, but

makes correlations where possible. In this case, three rows will be the output: John smith and his $100 balance, Frank Jones with no balance, and Account 345678 with a $150 balance but no name.

These four kinds of joins are one of the most powerful tools that relational databases have given us, but they also quickly lead to complexity. It is possible, for example, to take the resulting temporary table (called a "recordset") created by one of these joins and then join IT to still ANOTHER table. These chained joins can be repeated ad nauseum with no upper limit. This can grow very complicated very quickly.

Section 1.2: Indices & Keys

Speaking of rapidly increasing complexity... Our examples above are easy to make sense of, since they have only two rows each; but what about a table with ten thousand or even ten million rows? How quickly could *you* sort 1,000,000 names into alphabetical order? While a computer is significantly faster than you or I at such tasks, it is still often not fast *enough* without a little help, and this is where indexes come in. An index is sort of like a separate invisible column hanging alongside your data that keeps the names pre-alphabetized, the dollar amounts pre-sorted and those account numbers in the same order in table A as in table B. Now since they actually contain data, they *do* take up some disk space, so you typically don't want to index everything in every possible way, but failure to index a commonly used field can result in your database engine scanning through a million records, one at a time, looking for some arbitrary bit of data.

While indexing itself turns into a very complex topic very rapidly, there is one type of index worth specifically mentioning here, at the very beginning: The primary key. While some database engines will allow you to create a table with no primary key, nearly every table will (and should!) have one. A primary key is a special index that serves as the main identifier for a given record in a table – its value must be unique for every record and it typically affects the order in which the data is physically stored on the disc (although not *every* primary key is also the "clustered index" which defines physical storage order). In some cases, there may not be a single field which would be unique by itself. In this case, we can define a "Composite primary key" which references multiple columns of data which, in combination, will always be unique. One bank, for example, will allow the same username to exist multiple times, but only once per state; there may be a dozen copies of "dperry" in their "users" table, but only one can be from Nevada.

It is also possible to create a "foreign" key which references the primary key of another table. This is particularly important in scenarios involving a "one-to-many" or "many-to-one" relationship where one table contains, for example, an account ID and another table contains many historical records of what that account ID has done. In such a scenario, the historical data table would have to have a different primary key since, for this table, the account ID could not be unique. The historical data table could, however, have a foreign key for the account ID that refers to the primary key of the accounts table. This helps to enforce "referential integrity" – meaning that one could not delete an account without first deleting the historical data associated with it. If one were able to delete the account without first deleting its associated records from other tables, it can lead to what database administrators lovingly refer to as "orphaned records." They waste storage space, they waste processor cycles as the database engine needlessly scans through them and eventually they will waste your time as you hunt and peck to find them scattered throughout the database. Referential integrity is a very big important topic.

* * * *

Chapter 2: Microsoft SQL Server Basics

There are many different database technologies available on the market today, but this book will focus on the most commonly found database engine: Microsoft's SQL Server. We will make a brief foray into the free/open-source camp with a quick overview of MySQL but the differences covered by this book are little more than semantics (what Microsoft's SQL calls a "job" MySQL calls an "event" etc.). Once you have learned one SQL framework it is relatively easy to apply your knowledge to another. In this chapter we'll be going over a brief overview of general concepts. Most of these concepts will be explored in more detail, with examples, in later chapters.

Section 2.1: System Databases

Once you've mapped your first SQL server in Enterprise Manager (a process which is outside the scope of this book, but I assure you is quite simple) you may notice a few already-existing databases. You might be tempted, at first, to delete these in order to save space: please don't. Here is a brief overview of what you might find:

- Master
  This is Microsoft SQL's main database. It tracks and controls information about every other database on the SQL server including database listings, setup options, user processes, locking and user credentials.

- Model
  This database is the framework for building other databases. It is essentially a blank database with your specific options already set. Any time you

create a new database, what you're really doing is making a copy of Model.

- MSDB
  This database is used by SQL Server Agent to track both jobs and alerts (more on those later)

- TEMPDB
  This is a temporary storage area used to hold temporary tables and other temporary objects which require physical storage (i.e. recordsets larger than your available RAM)

You may also find a "Northwind" or "Pubs" database. These are mock databases that can be installed alongside SQL server, typically used for practice or demonstration purposes. If necessary, they may be deleted without consequence.

Section 2.2: The Interface

While the interface of Microsoft's SQL tools have changed somewhat over the years, the initial view upon opening Enterprise Manager or SQL Server Management Studio is much the same. You should see a two-paned view, with available/registered databases to the left and a mostly blank window to the right. Microsoft has gone to great lengths in all versions of this product to create a user-friendly interface, so I'll not spend a lot of time on navigation. The goal of this book is to teach general proficiency, not skill with a specific product. If you require such specific knowledge, far better to turn to the internet, especially since such data is highly version-specific.

Once you've browsed to and expanded an individual database, you're likely to see submenus which include something like the following:

- Tables
  This menu contains a list of all tables available in the database.

- Views
  Views are a special kind of stored procedure that look, behave and may be queried as though they were a table, but (quite importantly) are read only. These are commonly used for reports.

- Stored Procedures/Programmability
  Stored procedures are pre-written snippets of SQL code which can be executed by name, either manually or by a job.

- Security
  Here you'll find the various options concerning who may access which tables in the databases.

Within this interface you will also find tools for designing new tables visually, viewing and editing the contents of a table and many other useful functions, some of which we'll describe later; for now, let's right-click on a table and select "Design."

Section 2.3: Design View & Data Types

In design view we should see three columns, populated with data. The columns are "Column Name," "Data Type," and "Allow Nulls." Column name is the name of the field associated with a given column such as "Account ID" or "Customer Name" – while spaces are a valid character for both column and table names, they will make your life much more difficult later, so do your best to avoid them if possible. The second field, "Data Type," deserves some special explanation. SQL has many different ways of handling different kinds of data. If we add one to today's date, for example, we get tomorrow. If we add "1" to the character string "dog" we get "dog1" and if we add 1 to the number 4 we get 5. In order to properly handle your data, SQL needs to know what kind of data it is – and there are a lot of options! Here are some of the more common:

- Char(n)
  This is an alphanumeric data type that is fixed in length (n characters long). If n = 4 then char(n) will always be stored using exactly 4 bytes. If it is given data less than 4 characters long, it will be padded with spaces.

- Varchar(n)
  Varchar is identical to char except that it is not fixed in length. In the case of varchar(n), n specifies the maximum length of the data it may contain. If one passes a string less than n characters long, only the necessary bytes will be used to store the data.

- DateTime
  Stores dates in a date and time format. This can accept dates from Jan. 1, 1753 00:00:01.000 through Dec. 31, 9999 23:59:59.999. This field takes 8 bytes of space and has a maximum accuracy of 3.33 milliseconds.

- SmallDateTime
  Similar to DateTime, but uses less space (4 bytes) but only stores dates and times to a maximum accuracy of one minute. Valid dates are from Jan. 1, 1900 00:01 to Jun. 6, 2079 23:59.

- Int
  A numeric data type which can store any whole number from -2,147,483,648 to 2,147,483,648

- Smallint
  A numeric data type which can store any whole number from -32,768 to 32,768

- TinyInt
  A numeric data type which can store any whole number from 0 to 255

- Float
  A numeric data type which exists for numbers without a fixed decimal point. Values stored in a float are approximate and rounding will occur. Can store numbers from -1.79e+308 to 1.79e+308

- Real
  Real is similar to Float, but has a range of -3.40e+38 to 3.48e+38

- Money
  A numeric data type that stores up to 4 decimal places

- Numeric
  A numeric data type that can store any number with up to 38 digits, including numbers before and after the decimal point. Numeric is quite accurate and can deal with significantly larger/smaller numbers than the other numeric data types, but is slower to perform arithmetic functions with.

Finally, the "Allow Nulls" column is simply checkboxes. These checkboxes define whether that column can hold a "null" value or not. Null is the value that a variable holds before it is initialized – it is *not* equal to zero; zero is a value, null is the absence of a value. Essentially, the "Allow Nulls" column is asking whether a given column is mandatory. One other thing we might notice is that one column will have a tiny key icon next to it. This denotes the primary key for the table.

At the bottom of the design view window, you might see a properties dialog for the column you've currently got selected. There are a lot of options in this dialog, and you might use a few of them from time to time, but more often than not the only one you'll use is "Default Value or Binding." This property allows you to specify what data this column should hold if no other data is passed in.

Section 2.4: Views

Let's go ahead and close our design view window, opting not to save changes. If we right click on the "Views" folder and select "New View" we will be prompted to choose a number of tables to add to the view. If we select one or more tables, they will appear in the top portion of the multi-paned view designer window. Dragging one column onto another will indicate what columns these tables have in common and we can individual check columns from both tables that we would like to appear in the view and select how to sort them from this dialog as well. More commonly, though, sufficiently advanced users will forego these fanciful design windows and simply write their query out in the "SQL" pane, second from the bottom. We will explore SQL (structured query language) a bit more in another chapter, but for now simply know that the top two panes will rarely, if ever be used. In my working environment I've simply disabled them entirely.

Section 2.5: Stored Procedures

Similarly, if we find and right-click on the "Stored Procedures" folder and select "New Stored Procedure" we will be greeted with the design mode for stored procedures or "procs" as they are commonly called. For the first time in our explorations, what we are prompted with is actually precisely as complex as it appears. The stored procedure editor is merely a text editor window in which we type the SQL statements that make up our procedures. Stored procedures are full-blown SQL programming and will be discussed at great length in later chapters. For now, just be aware that a stored procedure can do practically anything that you can do, if written correctly.

Somewhere toward the bottom of your left-hand pane will be an option for "SQL Server Agent" – depending on your version it may be hidden within the "Management" folder. SQL Server Agent is responsible for "Jobs" and "Alerts." A job is sort of like a stored procedure that is attached to a schedule. In short, a stored procedure can do nearly anything, but it has to be explicitly executed by someone or something. Jobs are stored procedures that, according to a set of timing rules, can execute themselves. Alerts, on the other hand, are not timed but rather event-driven. An alert can execute a given piece of code when one of your log files becomes full or a certain kind of error occurs.

The last missing bit of this automation isn't in SQL Server Agent at all, but tucked away within menus or sub-nodes of a table, depending on your version. I'm talking about triggers. Where a job fires on a schedule and an alert fires on a database-wide circumstance, a trigger fires when a table is changed in a certain way. Triggers can watch for records to be inserted, updated or deleted from a table and take action under the right circumstances. With this final piece of the puzzle in place, SQL can begin to take on a life of its own, reacting to circumstances and actions. We have graduated from a simple database to a fully programmable data storage system.

With all of these self-firing functions it's easy for the system to run away with itself. That's why we should also be aware of good tools for basic monitoring of the server. In newer versions, you can find the activity monitor by right-clicking on the server in the left pane. In older versions, a "Current Activity" item was available from within the Management folder. Both new and old give a brief overview of the current state of the server, what processes are running, and what resources are locked.

* * * * *

Chapter 3: Maintenance & Management Tasks

Maintenance is an important topic in the database world. Without proper maintenance, data is likely to become corrupted and eventually lost. Not only this, but without structure behind the data even uncorrupted data will eventually become impossible to sort through in reasonable timeframes.

Section 3.1: DBCC

The first and most important of all SQL maintenance commands to understand is DBCC. DBCC stands for "Database Console Commands" and contains a number of sub-commands which check and repair the physical and logical consistency of a database. To use DBCC we simply type the command into a query analyzer window. The most common commands used with DBCC include:

- CheckTable

- CheckDB

- DBReindex

- IndexDefrag

The DBCC CheckTable command verifies that the specified table and/or its associated indices do not have any inconsistencies or corruption. The syntax for DBCC CheckTable is `DBCC CheckTable ('Table_Name')` to check the whole table or `DBCC CheckTable ('Table_Name', Index_ID)` to check a single index. To repair errors found with DBCC CheckTable, simply re-run the command which discovered the errors with one of the following appended:

- Repair_Fast
  Performs minor, non-time-consuming repairs such as repairing extra keys in non-clustered indices.

- Repair_Rebuild
  Performs all repairs done by Repair_Fast and also includes time-consuming repairs like rebuilding indices. Repair_Rebuild will not attempt repairs that could result in data loss.

- Repair_Allow_Data_Loss
  Performs all possible repairs, including those that could result in data loss.

In order for SQL to execute any of the above repair options, the database to be repaired must be in single-user mode. You can switch a database between single and multi user mode through its properties dialog or by executing the statement `ALTER DATABASE [DB_NAME] SET SINGLE_USER` – The database may be returned to multi-user mode with the statement `ALTER DATABASE [DB_NAME] SET MULTI_USER`.

The DBCC CheckDB command verifies all the tables in a database. This is useful for when multiple tables in your database may have issues, though it is often quite time consuming. The Syntax for CheckDB is simply `DBCC CheckDB` to check the current database or `DBCC CheckDB ('DB_NAME')` to check another database. CheckDB allows for the same repair modes with the same commands ad CheckTable and, similarly, the database in question must be in single-user mode.

DBReindex, as the name implies, is the DBCC command responsible for rebuilding one or more indices on a given table. The syntax for DBReindex is `DBCC`

`DBReindex('table_name', 'Index_Name')` to simply re-index according to the default values. When reindexing using DBCC you may also specify a fill factor. The fill factor of an index is the percentage of space on each index page to be used for storing data. The remainder will be kept blank, allowing space for new entries to enter the index without having to re-write every entry after the insertion point. High fill factors mean less time spent reading through the index pages. Low fill factors mean lots of free space for inserting new records. Depending on whether reading or writing is the most common function of a given table, values for Fill Factor range between 60 (best for writing) and 99 (best for reading). To specify a fill factor, we change the syntax to `DBCC DBReindex ('table_name', 'index_name', fillfactor)` where fillfactor is simply a number.

Finally, we have yet another nominee for the category of "most obviously descriptive name" – IndexDefrag. Just like files on your hard drive, entries in an index can get fragmented over time. Just like defragmenting files is the solution to the prior problem, defragmenting indices is the solution to the second. The syndex for IndexDefrag is `DBCC IndexDefrag ('db_name', 'table_name', 'index_name')`

Update Statistics is another highly important maintenance command. Statistics on all tables are stored in the Master database. These tables contain crucial data about indices, keys, pages, extents and much more. These stats are used by SQL to decide how best a query might be executed with the best performance. Accurate stats lead to accurate choices and faster queries. If this information becomes outdated, it will need to be updated. SQL does a pretty good job of this on its own, but sometimes it's worth a shot to force a stat update. We can do this by executing the oh-so-cryptic command `UPDATE STATISTICS table_name`. Or, if we'd like to update stats for the entire database, we have the somewhat more cryptic `EXEC SP_UPDATESTATS`.

Now once we've updated the statistics, we might not be done. Stored procedures, for example, are compiled with the most current stats available, but those compiled versions are cached for a time, and so without being recompiled, those cached versions will remain inefficient. Thankfully it's pretty easy to recompile those too: simply run `EXEC SP_RECOMPILE procedure_name` to recompile a single stored procedure. Unfortunately there is no prefabricated process for recompiling all stored procedures in a given database, but scripts to do so are readily available on the internet.

Section 3.2: Backups

A good part of any maintenance plan should be a backup of some kind. Regularly scheduled backups are easily done through jobs, third-party software or even SQL's own integrated backup manager. Unfortunately, the general consensus seems to be that Microsoft's built-in tools are inadequate for enterprise-level solutions and so the backup solutions you're likely to find in the field are varied enough to deserve their own book. I will, however, cover the different varieties of backups you're likely to encounter.

- Database / Full
  These terms are interchangeable and refer to a complete backup of every single bit and byte of your data. A full backup should include the various system databases, transaction logs, all data files, preferences, users and security settings. These are the best possible backups to have, but they are

also very time consuming and require huge volumes of storage space.

- Differential / Simple
Another set of interchangeable terms, we're now talking about backing up only that data which is new or different since our last backup. Assuming that your entire catalog of differential backups is undamaged back to your last full backup, you should suffer no data loss. Differential backups are often paired with less-frequent full backups; the full backups provide a worst-acceptable fallback point and the differential backups provide a fairly likely chance of a full restoration. Differential or Simple backups are less secure but far faster than full database backups.

- Transaction Log
This is something of a special point. The transaction log holds a record of logins, deletions, DBCC executions and so forth. The completeness of this log depends upon your individual server's settings. How it gets backed up is also dependent upon your server's settings. If you have your database's backup mode set to "Full" then the transaction log will grow forever, until it is manually trimmed or runs out of space. This means that each backup will contain a full copy of your transaction log back to the last deliberate truncation. "Simple" backup mode, on the other hand, wipes the transaction log clean at each and every backup. Which mode you choose depends on how important your transaction logs are to you. For most companies, they are important only from a short-term security standpoint – tracking logins is an easy way to catch a thief – but in some

industries, the transaction logs are quite important, or even legally regulated!

Aside from these active maintenance tasks, a fair portion of preventative maintenance is simply keeping an eye on things that *could* go wrong. You will want to keep an eye on the size of your databases, for example. Nothing spells disaster faster than a database that has run out of drive space! In SQL 2000 it was quite easy to get an overview of your space situation – simply click on a database and a TaskPad would appear with bar graphs showing the current file sizes and how much space was free. In newer versions, one must right click on a database and select an appropriate disk space report from the reports menu. The information is somewhat harder to obtain, but the quality of data in the reports is much higher.

Section 3.3: Performance Monitoring & Traces

Similarly, tools like Performance Monitor can be used to remotely monitor such things as CPU utilization, free memory and disk I/O. The specifics of remote hardware monitoring are, again, a topic with so many options that they deserve their own book, but Microsoft's own "Performance Monitor" software is quite functional and should be more than sufficient for most server monitoring tasks.

Should you find, through use of such performance monitoring tools, that your system is being inundated with requests, locked up or otherwise performing poorly, you might want to know how to run a trace. A SQL trace is a task designed to monitor the server's activity, filter out those events which meet certain criteria and display information about them.

While most of the functions of Query Analyzer and Enterprise Manager have been rolled into one interface in the newer versions of SQL, Profiler remains its own separate entity. To access it from either interface, old or new, simply select the

Profiler option from the Tools menu. In older versions, you will be presented with a multi-tabbed properties dialog in which you select the server you'd like to trace, whether and/or how you would like to store the results, what events you would like to log, what columns of data about those events you'd like to display and what filters you'd like to apply. Filters are of huge importance, since without filters you'd be sifting through all traffic to and from the server, which can be a massive amount of data. Also worth noting, if you choose to filter by duration (perhaps to find slow or long-running tasks) be aware that only "completed" events will have a duration. Filtering by duration on a trace that includes "SQL:BatchStarting" will result in far too many unfiltered results to be useful.

In newer versions, you will be presented with a somewhat similar dialog, except that the events and columns tabs have been combined into a single grid of checkboxes, and the filters tab is now a separate dialog, accessible via the "Column Filters" button.

Once you've set up your trace the way you'd like it, in either version, you click run and are presented with a scrolling window of transactions as they occur. Learning to filter this data down to a useable quantity is a skill difficult to learn except from practice, especially since different kinds of tasks can be more or less responsible for system slowdown in different environments. For the application I'm currently supporting, stored procedures are almost always the culprit, but in the past it has been more common to find a large insert or update gumming up the works – neither process would have been caught in the net laid to trap the other.

Finally, the last tool we'll discuss in our maintenance and management arsenal is the tuning advisor/wizard. Within SQL Profiler (via the tools menu) is an application referred to as either the "Index Tuning Wizard" or "Database Engine Tuning

Advisor" depending on your SQL version. This tool takes a trace as input and performs analysis on your tables and indices in an attempt to improve the efficiency of your database(s). It can suggest what indices should be built or rebuilt on your tables to best optimize your database(s) for your specific use(s). Use of these tools is fairly self-explanatory: simply provide the file or specify the table to which your trace results were sent, the database to be analyzed, and begin analysis. There are a number of advanced options including whether the application should consider changing your physical data structure, whether it can create new views to be queried in place of tables, etc.

Chapter 4: Basic Queries

So far we've discussed the basic ideas of what a database is as well as how to build and maintain them. What we have, thus far, neglected is what we can actually do with them. In order for our data to be of any use to us, we must be able to perform some kind of analysis and take actions on the basis of that analysis. SQL does, after all, stand for "Structured Query Language" so what good would it be to have SQL and not understand queries?

This chapter serves as a basic introduction to the simple data manipulation commands inherent to all variants of SQL: SELECT, INSERT, UPDATE and DELETE. These commands are the most basic necessary knowledge you need to manage the contents of one or more tables. Microsoft has, over the years, added some proprietary extensions to SQL which they call "SQL Transact" or T-SQL. T-SQL is a Turing-complete programming language with SQL as its basis and can do nearly anything that one would expect of a fully-featured programming language. It is similar, in a number of ways, to BASIC but with a handful of syntactic differences. T-SQL will be the subject of Chapter 6.

Section 4.1: The SELECT Statement & Clauses

The most common kind of SQL statement in most environments is the SELECT statement. As its name implies, it is used to select a given number or type of records from a database. We'll be spending a lot of time on SELECT, mostly because the clauses we can apply to SELECT also apply to

INSERT, UPDATE and DELETE so we won't *have* to spend as much time on them. The simplest possible SELECT statement looks like this:

```
SELECT * FROM table_name
```

First comes the keyword, "SELECT" which tells the database what kind of operation we'll be performing. Next comes "*" which is a wildcard meaning "everything." Then we have the "FROM" keyword which tells SQL that we're done specifying what we want and we're about to tell it where we want it from. Finally, we specify the table name from which to pull our records. The above statement will return all records from the table "table_name." If we had more specific demands, we could begin by specifying only what columns we would like. If we simply wanted to see all the first and last names in a table called "users" for example, we'd write something like:

```
SELECT FirstName, LastName FROM users
```

Here, instead of our asterisk wildcard, we've specified a couple of columns, separated by a comma. We could add more columns, separated by more commas if we wanted to. Now, though, we'd like to get really choosey. Now we only want to know the name of the user whose account_id is 123:

```
SELECT Firstname, Lastname FROM users
WHERE account_id = 123
```

The WHERE clause tells SQL that we're about to give it some filtering criteria. We follow it immediately with account_id = 123 to indicate that we only want records for that user whose account_id is 123.

But oh no! There's more than one result! I forgot to mention that when users change their information we keep the old record. There's a char(1) field called current_revision in this table that holds a 'Y' if we're looking at the current record and 'N' if we're looking at a historical record. Now our query looks something like this:

```
SELECT Firstname, Lastname FROM users
WHERE account_id = 123
AND current_revision = 'Y'
```

Pretty straightforward? By using the AND keyword we are specifying to SQL that both conditions must be true in order for a row to meet our criteria. If we had said OR instead it would return all rows where the account_id was 123 as well as every row with a current_revision of 'Y' – certainly not what we wanted! Also note that we did not surround the 'Y' in double quotes, but apostrophes or "single quotes" – SQL uses the double quote for delimited identifiers, which will rarely if ever find a place in your everyday queries. If you find the need to search for a string containing an apostrophe, use a double-apostrophe to "escape" the character, like so:

```
SELECT account_id FROM customers
WHERE name = 'John''s Bait Shop'
```

Now what if we wanted to look for three different account IDs? Well we could do it longhand like this:

```
SELECT Firstname, Lastname FROM users
WHERE (account_id = 123
OR account_id = 234
OR account_id = 345)
AND current_revision = 'Y'
```

Note the parenthesis. The parenthesis, just like in math, change the order of operations. We're telling SQL "check all three of these things first, and return results where any of them are true" then with our final AND we're saying "now take that result set and give me just those records where current_revision = 'Y'" – But this is still the long way. The easier, more proper way would look like this:

```
SELECT Firstname, Lastname FROM users
WHERE account_id IN (123, 234, 345)
AND current_revision = 'Y'
```

Simpler, right? The IN keyword allows us to compare a field to a list of values, separated by commas. This statement and the previous one are logically identical and will produce the same results, but the one using the IN keyword is significantly shorter.

So now we know how to find records when we know an exact value, but what if we're looking for a range of values – say, all the account_id's between 123 and 234? The answer is as easy as looking at the question:

```
SELECT Firstname, Lastname FROM users
WHERE account_id BETWEEN 123 AND 234
AND current_revision = 'Y'
```

We can also use other familiar comparison operators such as greater than, (>) less than (<), greater than or equal to (>=), less than or equal to (<=) and we can negate any piece of logic using the NOT keyword, like so:

```
SELECT Firstname, Lastname FROM users
WHERE account_id NOT BETWEEN 123 AND 234
AND current_revision = 'Y'
```

But what if we aren't looking at exact values, or even a range? What if we want to find some all the users whose first name begins with the letter J?

```
SELECT Firstname, Lastname FROM users
WHERE Firstname LIKE 'J%'
AND current_revision = 'Y'
```

The percent sign (%) is a wildcard that can stand in for any number of characters, so in the query above we're effectively telling SQL that we want only first names where the first letter is J, but any character after the J doesn't matter. This will return a lot of results.

```
SELECT Firstname, Lastname FROM users
WHERE Firstname LIKE 'J_'
AND current_revision = 'Y'
```

This on the other hand, will not. The underscore (_) is also a wildcard, but it is a substitute for one and only one character. The only way this will find results is if we have a "Jo" in our database.

```
SELECT Firstname, Lastname FROM users
WHERE Firstname LIKE 'J[aeiou]%'
AND current_revision = 'Y'
```

This odd-looking query actually has two wildcards in it. A sequence of letters between brackets ([]) indicates that only those letters may stand in for the actual value, so what we're asking for here is all names beginning with J, where the second letter is a vowel, and we don't care what comes after the 2nd letter. We could negate our bracketed wildcard thusly:

```
SELECT Firstname, Lastname FROM users
WHERE Firstname LIKE 'J[!aeiou]%'
AND current_revision = 'Y'
```

The exclamation mark tells SQL to reverse its logic, so now we will only get names beginning with J in which the second character is NOT a vowel.

How about looking for unique values? There must be an awful lot of "John" and "David" in this table, what if we want a list of first names but we don't want a thousand "John"s?

```
SELECT DISTINCT(Firstname) FROM users
```

The DISTINCT keyword tells SQL that we aren't interested in duplicates. Even if we have 30 Johns in the table, the name "John" will appear only once in the result set. Now let's try something a little more advanced...

```
SELECT FirstName, Count(Firstname) FROM
users
GROUP BY FirstName
```

A few new concepts are hiding in this one. First we've used an aggregate function: Count. Count does exactly what it sounds like, it counts things. If we had 432 records in the users table and ran

```
SELECT Count(*) FROM users
```

Our resulting recordset would contain the value 432. So we're obviously counting something here, but what is this GROUP BY thing? GROUP BY can be used in conjunction with aggregate functions to make them aggregate differently. In this case, we've told it to group by first name. SQL takes all the records in the users table and puts them into groups by first name – so all those Johns and Davids we talked about earlier are clumped together – then the Count() function counts them. If there are 22 Davids in the table, we'll end up with a row containing two values: David, 22. Similarly there will be rows to count all of the Johns and Franks and Jills and Stephanies. The other common aggregate functions are MIN(), MAX(), AVG() and SUM() which return the lowest, highest, average and total of a given field, respectively.

Finally, we might want to sort this data somehow sorted so that we can make sense of it. We want our count of first names sorted alphabetically, so let's try…

```
SELECT FirstName, Count(Firstname) FROM
users
GROUP BY FirstName
ORDER BY FirstName
```

The ORDER BY keyword tells SQL we would like our results alphabetized by the FirstName field. If we wanted to we could specify "ORDER BY FirstName ASC" or "ORDER BY FirstName DESC" to specify ascending (lowest to highest) or descending (highest to lowest) order. There's one more important note regarding the GROUP BY clause: it does not support the WHERE clause, instead we use HAVING:

```
SELECT FirstName, Count(Firstname) FROM
users
GROUP BY FirstName
ORDER BY FirstName
HAVING FirstName LIKE 'D%'
```

HAVING works exactly the same as WHERE, and supports all of the same comparison operators, it's just a slight syntax difference.

Section 4.2: Joins & Unions

So now that all of the easy stuff is out of the way… Let's look at Joins. We discussed Joins briefly in Chapter 1, so you should be familiar with the basic types of joins already (left, right, inner, outer). Let's put them into practice, shall we?

```
SELECT * FROM user_history
LEFT JOIN users
ON users.account_id =
user_history.account_id
```

Ok, so that might look a little complicated at first glance (because it is) but let's apply what we already know. A LEFT JOIN is a join in which the first table specified (user_history) is the important one that we want all the rows from and the second table (users) is the one we only want data from if it matches. The ON keyword is where we specify what we expect to match. There is an account_id field in both of these tables that should correspond to one another, so this query appears to be pulling all the data from user_history (which ostensibly contains multiple rows for each user) and tacking onto each row those records from users with a matching account_id. The clauses for the other joins (right, inner and outer) are, simply enough, RIGHT JOIN, INNER JOIN and OUTER JOIN.

But there is one more way to join two result sets together that we haven't discussed yet: the UNION keyword. Where joins try to staple two record sets together side-by-side, unions staple them top to bottom (or more accurately, when an ORDER BY clause is used, interleaves their records). Consider the following statement:

```
SELECT LastName, FirstName FROM users
UNION
SELECT LastName, FirstName FROM
customers
ORDER BY LastName
```

We've unioned the users and customers table together here. Note that we've selected the same number of columns from each table – this is a requirement of a union. This will give us a list of all first and last names from both tables, sorted alphabetically. If a name combination exists in both tables, by default it will be in the result set only once. If we want the name to show up once for each record regardless of duplicates, we would change our UNION into a UNION ALL.

Section 4.3: Insert, Update and Delete

Now that we know how to get records out of a database, it might be nice to know how to get them in, change them and eventually remove them. This is where the INSERT, UPDATE and DELETE statements come into play. With the exception of JOIN and UNION, the clauses we discussed for SELECT work just the same for the other commands so we won't need to cover them again.

```
INSERT INTO table_name
VALUES (val1, val2)
```

This query will insert a row into the specified table with the specified values. The values are specified in the order in which the fields appear in the table. If you do not want to specify all of the values (allowing some to be filled by defaults, for example) it might look more like this:

```
INSERT INTO table_name
(column1, column2)
VALUES (val1, val2)
```

Now let's have a look at UPDATE:

```
UPDATE table_name
SET column1=val1, column2=val2
WHERE column1=some_value
```

UPDATE looks a bit more like the SELECT statement we're accustomed to. We are telling SQL to change the value of "column1" to "val1" and "column2" to "val2" for every row where "column1" is equal to "some_value" – it's important to make sure that your WHERE clause(s) are accurately selecting only those records you want to change, so it might be worth writing this as a SELECT statement first just to be sure you're targeting the right rows.

```
DELETE FROM table_name
WHERE column1=some_value
```

DELETE is another simple one. Note that we don't specify any column names or even an asterisk between DELETE and FROM. This is because the DELETE command acts on an entire row at once – there is no way to delete a specific field; we can alter the table to no longer contain that field or we can update a given row, setting the value stored in that field to NULL, but we cannot DELETE it.

Section 4.4: Transactions

As a final note, I'd like to mention Transactions briefly. Transactions are the one and only "undo" in SQL and they must be explicitly used. There is no UNDELETE command, nor can you UNUPDATE the 80,000 records you just changed because your WHERE clause was faulty, the only way to stay safe with these two scary commands is within a transaction. Consider the following code:

```
BEGIN TRAN
DELETE FROM table_name
WHERE column1=val1
```

This code will produce a result that looks like any other delete statement, but with two important differences. The BEGIN TRAN at the top instructed SQL to hold off on actually making the changes, but to tell us what would happen if we did. Now if it says "3 records affected" and that's the number we were going for, we can execute a COMMIT command and the changes will be written. If, on the other hand, we end up with

3,000 records affected, we can issue a ROLLBACK command and save ourselves. Do note that depending on some settings, the table may be locked until either a COMMIT or ROLLBACK command is sent, so make your decisions quickly – no one else can use that table while you are in a transaction.

Section 4.5: Drop and Truncate

Now I've said this before but in this context it bears repeating: SQL DOES NOT HAVE AN UNDO COMMAND. Make absolutely sure you understand this before you *ever* type the words "DROP" or "TRUNCATE TABLE" into a query window. Each of these commands takes only one argument, the name of a database object, and does intentional, irreversible damage to that object. The DROP command removes an object from the database. The TRUNCATE TABLE command deletes the data from a table, but leaves the table itself intact. Let's see what they look like.

```
DROP TABLE employees
TRUNCATE TABLE customers
```

Scarily simple commands to be so powerful and so dangerous. Again, never type these words unless you are 100% certain of what you're doing, and even then, if possible, only type them immediately after a backup.

*****

Chapter 5: Advanced Queries

What we covered in Chapter 4 are the bare basics – the stuff you need just to be functional in a SQL-driven world. There are more advanced concepts that will allow you to be really proficient without actually taking SQL to the extremes we'll be learning in Chapter 6.

Section 5.1: Nested Queries

One of the most common types of advanced queries you might encounter are nested queries. Consider the following:

```
SELECT DISTINCT(account_id)
FROM order_history
WHERE order_amount > 100.00
```

This query would return a list of account IDs for all customers who have placed a single order worth more than $100.00, but assuming the customer's name isn't in the order_history table, how do we use this list of account IDs to create a list of names? We could certainly perform a JOIN, but that's not always the most efficient way of doing things and in some cases isn't even really feasible. Let's have a look at how a SQL pro might solve this problem:

```
SELECT FirsName, LastName
FROM customers
WHERE account_id IN (
  SELECT DISTINCT(account_id)
  FROM order_history
  WHERE order_amount > 100.00
)
```

What we've done here is use our original query as the list portion of an IN clause. Why would we want to do this? Imagine for a moment what would happen if we tried to join two tables on a field that, in one of them, was not indexed. Without an index to expedite the sorting and seeking process, SQL would revert to a method called the "Full Table Scan." A table scan requires SQL to go through the entirety of both tables one record at a time looking for matches. Table scans take a long time, comparatively speaking, and are the least efficient possible way to find information. If this were a one-time query or a process that occurred only occasionally, it would not be worthwhile for us to add an index to a large table. If order_history were indexed on order_amount but not on account_id, a join would be the least efficient possible way to get this information. Nested queries allow us to phrase our statements in such a way that we should always be able to avoid table scans.

Section 5.2: Seeks & Scans

But how do you know if you're going to cause a table scan? Under the Query menu you'll find an option titled "Display Estimated Execution Plan" (Ctrl+L) that will display the steps that SQL is likely to go through when completing your query. SQL has many ways of searching a table, here are a few of the more common ones in order from best to worst efficiency:

- Clustered Index Seek

- Index Seek

- Clustered Index Scan

- Index Scan

- Table Scan

So, in general, a seek is better than a scan and it's always better to do something on an indexed field than to the whole table. The clustered index is the index which determines the physical order in which records are stored on the disk and so will be slightly more efficient than a regular index seek/scan. The degree to which the clustered index is more efficient is largely dependent upon your server's storage hardware.

An index seek is more efficient than a scan because it only touches rows that qualify for your criteria and only touches the pages which contain those rows. The presence of a good index allows SQL to skip over data that is simply unrelated to your query. Be aware that some aggregate functions and certain other advanced practices can make indices unusable. The following query, for example, will cause an index scan:

```
SELECT COUNT(*)
FROM order_history
```

There might not seem, at first, to be an alternative way to find this information but in fact there are several. This for instance:

```
SELECT row_count
FROM sys.dm_db_partition_stats
WHERE OBJECT_NAME(OBJECT_ID) =
'order_history'
```

Which brings us to our next topic in advanced SQL...

Section 5.3: Using the System Tables

SQL has a number of built-in system-level tables that have extremely useful information. The most commonly used of these tables are sysobjects and syscolumns.

Sysobjects contains a list of all "objects" known to the system. From SQL's perspective this can mean a lot of things. If we were looking only for tables, for example, we might run this query:

```
SELECT * FROM sysobjects
WHERE xtype = 'U'
```

The 'U' stands for "user table" (as opposed to the system tables, such as sysobjects) so this query should return all of the non-system tables. Here is a list of possible values for xtype:

- C: CHECK constraint

- D: DEFAULT constraint

- F: FOREIGN KEY constraint

- L: Log

- P: Stored Procedure

- PK: PRIMARY KEY constraint

- RF: Replication filter stored procedure

- S: System tables

- TR: Triggers

- U: User table

- UQ: UNIQUE constraint

- V: Views

- X: Extended stored procedure

- TF: Functions

That's quite a few values, and unfortunately there's no easier way to remember these than a cheat sheet. Fortunately, you won't often use most of these – knowing U, P and V should suffice for most tasks.

Our next system table is syscolumns. Where sysobjects holds the top-level items like tables, syscolumns lets us drill down and look at specific columns in our tables. A query to syscolumns might look like this:

```
SELECT * FROM syscolumns
WHERE name LIKE 'account%'
```

In this example , we're looking for any column in any table with a name that begins with account. But there's something missing...

```
SELECT OBJECT_NAME(id), *
FROM syscolumns
WHERE name LIKE 'account%'
```

That's better. By default, the only field in syscolumns that identifies the table a given column belongs to is the ID field, which is a unique numeric identifier – unless you want to memorize a lot of numbers, we need some way to tie these two together. We could join syscolumns to sysobjects on the ID field, and that would certainly work, but it's not necessary. SQL has provided us with the system function OBJECT_NAME() which converts IDs into names anywhere we find them.

The rest of the syscolumns table is pretty self-explanatory – with one minor exception: xtype. In sysobjects, xtype had a handful of values and they were one or two letter combinations that, if we had to, we could easily memorize. In syscolumns, xtype is suddenly numeric – and there are a LOT of numbers!

In syscolumns, xtype identifies the data type of a given column. If you need to look up a column that has a specific data type, there is one more system table you might find handy: systypes. Consider the following query:

```
SELECT xtype, name FROM systypes
```

This query will return the numeric xtype value and the friendly name we're accustomed to for every type currently supported by your server.

Section 5.4: Switching Databases

The USE keyword allows us to switch from one database context to another within the execution of a query. If, for example, our customers table and our employees table were not just in different tables but actually in different databases (on the same server) a report incorporating data from both databases might look something like this:

```
USE employees
SELECT * FROM employee_names
USE customers
SELECT * FROM customer_names
```

This is simple enough, but not always convenient. Everything between one USE statement and the next will be executed on whatever database the USE statement specified. If we've got a rather complicated report we might have to switch back and forth several times. It's also not possible to JOIN tables across databases in this manner. To perform a JOIN or simply handle context switching in a more agile manner, we'll have to learn a bit about object-oriented programming.

The basic concept of object-oriented programming is to stop treating things like separate variables randomly dropped across the code landscape and start treating things like objects.

Objects have properties: this apple is red. Objects have functions: this knife cuts things. In object-oriented programming we talk about objects that have subobjects: My body has arms, my arms have hands and my hands have fingers. So how do we switch contexts in an object-oriented way? Here's the same query again:

```
SELECT * FROM
employees.dbo.employee_names
SELECT * FROM
customers.dbo.customer_names
```

So now instead of specifying the database in the USE command, we specify it where we normally put a table name. What we're really doing is giving SQL navigational directions to the table we want. Employees.dbo.employee_names really means "start at the employees database, navigate to the database object collection (dbo) and find the object called 'employee_names.'" Since in this manner we can work with multiple tables without the need to execute a USE command and break the flow of our code, something like this becomes possible:

```
SELECT * FROM customers.dbo.orders c
LEFT JOIN employees.dbo.employee_names e
ON c.employee_id = e.teller_id
```

Speaking of which...

Section 5.5: Aliases

Much of the time, shortcuts are a bad thing; they make your code illegible and all but the indoctrinated few who know the trick you just used are now incapable of deciphering what you've done. Sometimes, however, shortcuts are necessary; they can keep your code brief, concise and legible. In SQL one such type of shortcut is an alias. Let's look at that cross-database SELECT again.

```
SELECT * FROM customers.dbo.orders c
LEFT JOIN employees.dbo.employee_names e
ON e.employee_id = c.teller_id
```

On the first and second lines, we've done something new: we've told SQL that for the duration of this SELECT statement, we'd like to refer to 'customers.dbo.orders' as the letter 'c' and we'd like to refer to 'employees.dbo.employee_names' as the letter 'e.' Why would we want to do this? Let's have a look at that query without aliases.

```
SELECT * FROM customers.dbo.orders
LEFT JOIN employees.dbo.employee_names
ON
employees.dbo.employee_names.employee_id
= customers.dbo.orders.teller_id
```

Look at that last line! Because we're specifying the entire DBO path to a given object, things can get lengthy quite fast. Aliases are also handy for those times when the DBA who came before you made a table named "TableWhereWeStoreCustomerData" or other such madness.

But this is not the only thing a DBA might mean when using the term 'alias.' There is another type of alias available in SQL, different in utility. Previously we've used an alias to give something a shorter name, but what if we're looking at something that has no name at all? If we run this query:

```
SELECT Count(*) FROM employees
```

We might get something like this for a result:

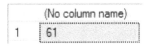
Figure 5.1: No column name

The heading "(No column name)" sits where a column name would typically go. In this case we've used an aggregate function and haven't told SQL what to call the resulting value, so it's defaulted to NULL. So let's fix that.

```
SELECT Count(*) AS num_employees FROM
employees
```

Now we've specified a name for our aggregate function and we'll get these results:

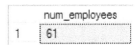
Figure 5.2: Alias as column name

Much better. Now the first query was pretty simple, so setting an alias might not have been strictly necessary, but as your queries grow more and more complex with more aggregate outputs, at what number of outputs will *you* lose track of which is which?

Section 5.6: Comments

Speaking of increasingly complex queries, at some point you'll write something so complex that you'll need a way to explain to others (or remind yourself) just what it is you're doing. This is where comments come in. Comments are lines within a query that will not be executed. They are explicitly in place only for the benefit of a human reader and are completely ignored by SQL. There are two ways to create a comment. To create a single-line comment, prefix it with two dashes:

```
-- Calculate the number of employees
SELECT Count(*) FROM employees
```

To create a multi-line comment you begin it with '/*' and end it with '*/' like so:

```
/* Calculate the number of employees
currently in the 'employees' table */
SELECT Count(*) FROM employees
```

Within SQL's query editor, comments will be displayed in green and as such should be easily distinguishable from the surrounding executable code.

Section 5.7: The TOP Keyword

The TOP keyword is used to pull only a given portion of data from the database. Its default functionality is to show only the first n records of the resulting recordset. Consider the following:

```
SELECT TOP 5 * FROM employees
```

This query will return only the first five records from the employees table. This is typically used in conjunction with an ORDER BY clause to return the highest or lowest valued row for a given field.

```
SELECT TOP 3 * FROM employees
ORDER BY totalsales DESC
```

This query will show the three employees with the highest total sales amounts. If we were to change the sort order to ASC (lowest to highest) it would display the three employees with the lowest sales. If we were doing more statistical analysis we could perhaps modify our query a bit...

```
SELECT TOP 5 PERCENT * FROM employees
ORDER BY totalsales DESC
WITH TIES
```

In this query we've used the PERCENT keyword to tell SQL that we'd like to see the top 5% of employees as opposed to simply the top 5. The WITH TIES keyword indicates that if six people are tied for last place, we'd like to see all six of them. Without the WITH TIES keyword, our six-way tie might be cut off after 2 or 3 employees if the resulting record set would contain more than 5% of the total number of employees.

Section 5.8: Select Into

The INTO keyword modifies a SELECT statement such that it will create a new table containing the results of the query.

```
SELECT TOP 3 *
INTO top_employees
FROM employees
ORDER BY totalsales DESC
```

This query will take the results of our previous "top 3 employees" query and create a new table for them called "top_employees." Note that if you try to run this query a second time, it will produce an error. The INTO keyword can only be used to create a new table. If we wanted to insert these records again, we would have to run something like this:

```
INSERT INTO top_employees (
  SELECT TOP 3 *
  FROM employees
  ORDER BY totalsales DESC
)
```

A SELECT statement nested within an INSERT statement, as we briefly discussed in Section 5.1.

Section 5.9: Views (again)

As previously mentioned, views are pre-defined SELECT statements typically used for reporting purposes. We looked briefly at how to create a view through design view and I hinted that this was, perhaps, the least effective way to create a view once you knew a little SQL. Let's take our "top 5% of employees" query and turn it into a view.

```
CREATE VIEW top_5_percent AS
SELECT TOP 5 PERCENT * FROM employees
ORDER BY totalsales DESC
WITH TIES
```

Easier than design view now that you know what you're doing, right? Now instead of reproducing that SELECT statement in its entirety any time we need that list we can simply SELECT * FROM top_5_percent to get the same data.

Typically, views are used for reports, but that doesn't necessarily require that they be read-only. Under very few circumstances will you be able to INSERT to a view, and so it's probably best if you simply assume that you can't. Updating a view, however, can be done so long as you're not trying to update the result of an aggregate function. If you write an UPDATE statement that targets a view, the records in the tables referenced by that view will themselves be updated.

Section 5.10: Stored Procedures (again)

As previously mentioned, stored procedures are a method of storing code so that it can be re-used. In Chapter 6 we'll be going over Transact SQL, which turns stored procedures from mildly useful into monstrously powerful, but to appreciate the power of Transact we must first have a basic understanding of the stored procedure.

```
CREATE PROCEDURE proc_name AS
BEGIN
  /* Code comprising your stored
  procedure goes here */
END
```

The above code is the most basic framework for creating a stored procedure. Line one tells SQL to create a procedure named 'proc_name' and the BEGIN and END lines tell SQL, appropriately enough, where the procedure begins and ends. BEGIN and END are generic commands that, as we'll learn in Chapter 6, define the beginning and ending of many things. If we later wanted to run the code we stored in proc_name we would simply run:

```
EXEC proc_name
-- or you can run
EXECUTE proc_name
```

Almost no one type out the full word "execute" any more. It is worthy of note that there is nothing special about the EXEC command that prevents it from being used within another stored procedure. In this way, higher-level procedures may rely on lower-level procedures and we can efficiently re-use as much of our code as possible. If we want to change the contents of a stored procedure, we may either DROP it and CREATE it again, or we can use the ALTER PROCEDURE command, which has the same syntax as CREATE PROCEDURE.

If, for some reason, you don't want others to stumble upon your code, you may add the "WITH ENCRYPTION" option to your CREATE PROCEDURE command like so:

```
CREATE PROCEDURE proc_name WITH
ENCRYPTION AS
BEGIN
  /* Code comprising your stored
  procedure goes here */
END
```

Take note that there is no method inherent to SQL to easily decrypt an encrypted procedure. For this reason you will want to store a plain-text copy of any procedures created with encryption in a safe place, should you need to change or re-create them later. There are third-party tools and scripts, but they should be considered a last result as they do not always work precisely as desired.

*****

Microsoft (among others) has taken it upon themselves to extend the basic capabilities of SQL into a Turing-complete programming language. TSQL includes logic-branching structures, loops, a full library of mathematical operators, variables and much more. This chapter will by no means be an exhaustive list of TSQL features, but it should contain everything you need to write basic scripts. Since this book is targeted at IT professionals, we will be writing under the assumption that you understand the basic principles of programming (i.e. what a variable is) and will not go into detailed explanations of such topics. Even within such a limited scope, there is a lot to know about TSQL, so buckle up – it's going to be a very long chapter.

Section 6.1: Variables

Variables are the backbone of programming, without them we couldn't do much. TSQL supports variables of the same types available for fields, so what we might recognize as a "string" SQL would refer to as a "varchar" and so on. A brief list of commonly used data types can be found in Section 2.3 and a complete list of standard data types follows this paragraph, direct from Microsoft's web site (http://msdn.microsoft.com/en-us/library/aa258271(v=sql.80).aspx)

- **Integers**

    o Bigint
      Integer (whole number) data from -2^63 (-9,223,372,036,854,775,808) through 2^63-1 (9,223,372,036,854,775,807).

    o Int
      Integer (whole number) data from -2^31 (-

2,147,483,648) through 2^31 - 1
(2,147,483,647).

- o Smallint
  Integer data from -2^15 (-32,768) through
  2^15 - 1 (32,767).

- o Tinyint
  Integer data from 0 through 255.

- o Bit
  One bit, integer data with a value of 0 or 1

- **Decimal and Numeric**

  - o Decimal
    Fixed precision and scale numeric data from -
    10^38 +1 through 10^38 −1.

  - o Numeric
    Functionally equivalent to decimal.

  - o Money and SmallMoney

    - Money
      Monetary data values from -2^63 (-
      922,337,203,685,477.5808) through
      2^63 - 1 (+922,337,203,685,477.5807),
      with accuracy to a ten-thousandth of a
      monetary unit.

    - Smallmoney
      Monetary data values from -
      214,748.3648 through +214,748.3647,
      with accuracy to a ten-thousandth of a
      monetary unit.

- **Approximate Numerics**

- Float

  Floating precision number data with the following valid values: -1.79E + 308 through -2.23E - 308, 0 and 2.23E + 308 through 1.79E + 308.

- Real

  Floating precision number data with the following valid values: -3.40E + 38 through -1.18E - 38, 0 and 1.18E - 38 through 3.40E + 38.

- **Datetime and Smalldatetime**

  - Datetime

    Date and time data from January 1, 1753, through December 31, 9999, with an accuracy of three-hundredths of a second, or 3.33 milliseconds.

  - Smalldatetime

    Date and time data from January 1, 1900, through June 6, 2079, with an accuracy of one minute.

- **Character Strings**

  - Char

    Fixed-length non-Unicode character data with a maximum length of 8,000 characters.

  - Varchar

    Variable-length non-Unicode data with a maximum of 8,000 characters.

  - Text

    Variable-length non-Unicode data with a maximum length of 2^31 - 1 (2,147,483,647) characters.

- **Unicode Character Strings**

  - nChar
    Fixed-length Unicode data with a maximum length of 4,000 characters.

  - nVarchar
    Variable-length Unicode data with a maximum length of 4,000 characters. sysname is a system-supplied user-defined data type that is functionally equivalent to nvarchar(128) and is used to reference database object names.

  - nText
    Variable-length Unicode data with a maximum length of $2^{30} - 1$ (1,073,741,823) characters.

- **Binary Strings**

  - Binary
    Fixed-length binary data with a maximum length of 8,000 bytes.

  - varBinary
    Variable-length binary data with a maximum length of 8,000 bytes.

  - Image
    Variable-length binary data with a maximum length of $2^{31} - 1$ (2,147,483,647) bytes.

- **Other Data Types**

  - Cursor
    A reference to a cursor

  - Sql_variant
    A data type that stores values of various SQL

Server-supported data types, except text, ntext, timestamp, and sql_variant.

- o Table
  A special data type used to store a result set for later processing.

- o Timestamp
  A database-wide unique number that gets updated every time a row gets updated.

- o Uniqueidentifier
  A globally unique identifier (GUID).

Many of these data types are self-explanatory, some are not. Some will be explained within the scope of this chapter, some will not. I have only included this list as reference material and to perhaps portray what a large topic TSQL is, that so many pages could be dedicated to data types alone.

Of course, even if we memorized all of these data types (which very few people have) we still need to know how to create a variable and use it. Thankfully, it's pretty simple:

```
DECLARE @weeklypay smallmoney
```

Here we've created a variable called @weeklypay. All variables in SQL begin with an @ (at) sign, and a handful of system variables exist, predefined, that begin with a double-at (@@) sign. We briefly discussed @@rowcount earlier, to cite one example.

Now that we've got a variable, let's see how to use it.

```
SET @weeklypay = 500.00
-- or
SELECT @weeklypay = 500.00
```

So we can use both SET and SELECT to store a value in a variable. What's the difference? Well, there are a few key points.

- SET is the ANSI standard for variable assignment

- SET can assign one and only one variable, while with SELECT we could assign multiple, for example: `SELECT @weeklypay = 500.00, @hourlypay = 16.00`

- If we're assigning the results of a query to a variable, SET will enforce only one value to a variable and will throw an error if more than one value is returned by the query. SELECT will populate the variable with whatever result occupies the first row and throw no errors. Good luck troubleshooting that!

- Again, when assigning from a query, if the recordset is empty, SET will assign the variable the NULL value, while SELECT will do nothing at all – the variable will retain whatever value it held before the SELECT. Again, good luck troubleshooting.

Which is better? Well neither, really. As long as you're aware of the differences and can choose between the two intelligently and correctly, SET and SELECT have similar performance, similar syntax and are, for the most part, fairly interchangeable.

As we mentioned in our SET vs. SELECT list above, variables can also be set from the results of a query, like so:

```
DECLARE @weeklypay smallmoney
DECLARE @employeeid smallint
```

```
SET @employeeid = 123
SET @weeklypay = (
  SELECT TOP 1 payrate
  FROM employees
  WHERE employee_id = @employeeid
)
```

The same query, using SELECT instead of SET would look like this:

```
DECLARE @weeklypay smallmoney
DECLARE @employeeid smallint
SET @employeeid = 123
SELECT @weeklypay =
  TOP 1 payrate
  FROM employees
  WHERE employee_id = @employeeid
```

In the above statements, we also demonstrate how to declare and set SQL variables as well as how to set a SQL variable from the results of a SELECT statement. The SELECT statement itself also contains a variable, @employeeid, which we set on line 3.

Section 6.2: Branching Logic

Branching logic is one of the basic functions of any programming language. It provides us with the ability to compare things and take different actions on the basis of those comparisons. The most basic implementation of branching logic is the IF/ELSE IF/ELSE structure that exists in nearly every programming language and so, of course, exists in TSQL. Here is an example:

```
IF @number > 100 PRINT 'Big number'
ELSE IF @number < 10 PRINT 'Small
```

```
number'
ELSE PRINT 'Medium number'
```

So if we're doing something very simple then we can put the thing we want to do on the same line as the IF/ELSE IF/ELSE line. We could also put the statements one line below and they'd still work, like this:

```
IF @number > 100
   PRINT 'Big number'
ELSE IF @number < 10
   PRINT 'Small number'
ELSE
   PRINT 'Medium number'
```

But what if what we want to do requires two statements? Will this work?

```
IF @number > 100
   PRINT 'Big number'
   SET @numsize = 'Big'
ELSE IF @number < 10
   PRINT 'Small number'
   SET @numsize = 'Small'
ELSE
   PRINT 'Medium number'
   SET @numsize = 'Medium'
```

The short answer is no, it will not. SQL is not sophisticated enough, even with the TSQL additions, to handle multiple lines without a BEGIN and END. SQL will interpret line 2 as being governed by the IF on line 1. Line 3 will be executed regardless of what is stored in @number, and finally line 4 will cause a syntax error since SQL sees it as an ELSE IF without a matching IF. The correct syntax for the above query is this:

```
IF @number > 100
BEGIN
```

```
    PRINT 'Big number'
    SET @numsize = 'Big'
END
ELSE IF @number < 10
BEGIN
    PRINT 'Small number'
    SET @numsize = 'Small'
END
ELSE
BEGIN
    PRINT 'Medium number'
    SET @numsize = 'Medium'
END
```

This code will execute properly and follow the appropriate logic branches. Another way to handle logical branching in TSQL is the CASE statement. Its syntax is as follows:

```
SELECT 'Gender' = CASE
    WHEN @male_female = 'M' THEN 'Male'
    WHEN @male_female = 'F' THEN 'Female'
    ELSE 'Unknown'
END
```

The above code takes a simple M/F/Null gender specifier and expands it into friendlier text, but it could just as easily set variables, execute stored procedures or do anything else that SQL is capable of. CASE also supports multi-line branches in the same way that IF does, using BEGIN and END to delimit where one WHEN clause ends and the next begins. Note that CASE does not require a BEGIN of its own (the BEGIN is implied by the word CASE). Indentation is your friend when dealing with such logic, as a mismatched number of BEGIN and END clauses can happen easier than you think.

Section 6.3: GO

The GO statement is largely misunderstood and because its omission can cause errors while its unnecessary inclusion usually does not, it ends up being over-used at an alarming rate. Within the ANSI C-92 SQL standard, there are several statements which cannot be executed within a single batch. CREATE VIEW and DROP VIEW, for example, cannot be part of the same batch, so if you want to drop a view and then create a new one with the same name, it would have to look like this:

```
DROP VIEW top_5_percent
GO
CREATE VIEW top_5_percent AS
SELECT TOP 5 PERCENT * FROM employees
ORDER BY totalsales DESC
WITH TIES
```

The GO keyword tells SQL to stop where it is, execute what it's done so far as one batch and then begin a new batch. We don't need a GO at the end of this query because a GO is always implied to be the final line of any query.

Section 6.4: Input & Output Variables

Stored procedures are pretty powerful with what we know already, but sometimes they need to be given some information when they are called. If I want to fire one of my employees for example, I might need a procedure like this:

```
CREATE PROCEDURE FireEmployee
  @employee_id int
AS
BEGIN
  UPDATE employees
  SET active = 'N'
  WHERE id = @employee_id
END
```

On line 2, we declare a variable called @employee_id as an integer. Later in the procedure we use that variable, but nowhere in the procedure do we ever set it. This is because when this procedure is called, it will be called like this:

```
EXEC FireEmployees 123
```

The value '123' will be passed into the @employee_id variable when the EXEC statement is called. But what if no value is called? Well we can start by specifying a default value for the variable like so...

```
CREATE PROCEDURE FireEmployee
  @employee_id int = NULL
AS
BEGIN
  UPDATE employees
  SET active = 'N'
  WHERE id = @employee_id
END
```

But that doesn't totally solve the problem since there might be records in the employees table with a null id and we probably don't want to fire all of them if we don't call this proc properly, so the final proc should look like this:

```
CREATE PROCEDURE FireEmployee
  @employee_id int = NULL
AS
BEGIN
  IF @employee_id IS NOT NULL
  BEGIN
    UPDATE employees
    SET active = 'N'
    WHERE id = @employee_id
  END
END
```

If we need more than one input parameter, we separate them with commas. We can place them on separate lines if that makes the code more legible, but the commas must still be there:

```
CREATE PROCEDURE FireEmployee
  @employee_id int = NULL,
  @termination_date smalldatetime
AS
BEGIN
  IF @employee_id IS NOT NULL
  BEGIN
    UPDATE employees
    SET active = 'N',
    firedate = @termination_date
    WHERE id = @employee_id
  END
END
```

What if we want to return some output from our stored procedure? Say we want a procedure that looks up an employee by ID number and returns their full name, it might look something like this:

```
CREATE PROCEDURE FindName
  @employee_id int = NULL,
  @employee_name varchar(50) OUTPUT
AS
BEGIN
  SELECT @employee_name =
  FirstName + ' ' + LastName
  FROM employees
  WHERE id = @employee_id
END
```

The OUTPUT keyword tells SQL that the variable we just specified is not meant to pass data into the proc but rather to return the results of the proc. When the proc finishes executing, whatever value is in that variable will be returned as the output of the proc. We can do things like this:

```
DECLARE @eName varchar(50)
EXEC FindName 123, @eName OUTPUT
```

And now the full name found by the FindName proc is stored in the @eName variable. In this way, procs may call procs which themselves call procs. We can even create recursive procs – procs which, under the right circumstances, EXEC themselves.

Section 6.5: Arithmetic Operators

Math is a big part of why we use computers. Databases weren't really designed to do math like their cousin, the spreadsheet, but once you ad full programmability to the SQL language, the desire and need for arithmetic suddenly arise. TSQL supports most of the standard arithmetic operators we've come to expect from a programming language. The supported basic operators are, in order of precedence:

- Multiplication (*)

- Division (/)

- Modulo (%)

- Addition (+)

- Subtraction (-)

Note that we've got a missing member from the list – SQL does not support raising a number to a power via the traditional x^y notation. Rather, it has a built-in procedure whose syntax is:

```
POWER(x, y)
```

Where x is the base number and y is the power to which we are raising it. The output of POWER() is of the type 'float.' We also have use of parenthesis to change order of operations as per standard mathematics rules.

Another noteworthy point is that, when doing arithmetic with variables, the output will, unless otherwise specified, be of the same type as the variables being worked upon. Take the following code for example:

```
DECLARE @x int
DECLARE @y int
SET @x = 1
SET @y = 4
PRINT @x / @y
```

The above code will print '0' which we all know is not equivalent to ¼. The reason why is that the output of an integer divided by an integer will itself be an integer, which cannot store decimal portions. If we wanted this to output correctly we would have to either declare @x and @y as float or some other decimal data type or we could do this:

```
DECLARE @x int
DECLARE @y int
DECLARE @z float
SET @x = 1
SET @y = 4
SET @z = @x / @y
PRINT @z
```

By storing the result in a float, we could force SQL to give us the desired result of 0.25. We could also achieve this effect without a third variable thusly:

```
DECLARE @x int
DECLARE @y int
SET @x = 1
```

```
SET @y = 4
PRINT CAST(@x AS FLOAT) / @y
```

The CAST function converts from one data type to another, in this case from int to float. As long as one of the variables in the division problem is a float, the output will be a float. We could also use the CONVERT keyword like so:

```
DECLARE @x int
DECLARE @y int
SET @x = 1
SET @y = 4
PRINT CONVERT(FLOAT, @x) / @y
```

The CONVERT keyword is identical to the CAST keyword except in a few specific scenarios. The primary difference is that CONVERT allows for formatting, while cast does not. Take the following example:

```
DECLARE @d datetime
SET @d = '2011-05-13 12:00:00'
PRINT CONVERT(varchar(10), @d, 108)
```

In the above example, we're converting the datetime variable @d to a varchar. In this case we've given the CONVERT statement a third argument for formatting. The '108' specification returns only a time, so the output of this script will be '12:00:00.' There are 20 distinct styles for converting datetime to varchar alone. There are also styles for converting float, real, money, smallmoney etc. These quite numerous so I will not depict them here, but rather refer you to the official MSDN article: http://msdn.microsoft.com/en-us/library/aa226054

We can also use arithmetic to stand in place of a column value in a SELECT statement. Simply place the arithmetic in the fields list between the SELECT and FROM clauses and give it an AS alias if you'd like:

```
SELECT PurchaseAmt, PaidAmt,
PurchaseAmt - PaidAmt AS OwedAmt
FROM invoices
WHERE customer_id = 123
```

The above query calculates the amount still owed for a given customer based on the amount purchased and the amount paid, simple subtraction.

Section 6.6: Aggregate Functions (again)

We briefly mentioned aggregate functions and even gave a demonstration of the COUNT() function. There are several aggregate functions to choose from, however, and they are all in sufficiently common use as to deserve their own individual mentions.

- Avg
  Computes the average (arithmetic mean) of a group of numbers. Only works with numeric input

- Count
  Computes the number of records in a given set/group. Works with any type of input

- Max
  Computes the largest value in a given set/group. Works with char, numeric or datetime data types. In the case of datetime data types, computes the latest date in the set.

- Min
  Computes the smallest value in a given set/group.

Works with char, numeric or datetime data types. In the case of datetime data types, computes the oldest date in the set.

- Rank
  Returns the ordinal position of the row in the overall list. Works with any data type, but most useful with sorted data.

- Sum
  Computes the sum (total) of all values in a given set/group. Only works with numeric data types.

Section 6.7: Date Functions

Date Functions are a very important function in many SQL implementations. Often you'll find tables that have a time stamp of some kind and you'll need to query based on that time stamp. Often queries involving timestamps are security-related and so it's probably in your best interest to know how to manipulate datetime values quite well.

Just as importantly, you'll need to know how to create a timestamp field. I assure you it's quite simple; when creating your table, simply create a field of type datetime and set its default value to GetDate(). It's that easy. The system procedure GetDate() returns the current date and time as a full-sized datetime value, accurate to 3.33 milliseconds. If you add or subtract an integer number from GetDate() or, for that matter any datetime or smalldatetime variable, your result will be a timestamp precisely that many days plus or minus the current date; e.g. GetDate() + 1 is tomorrow and GetDate() – 1 is yesterday.

Aside from the very simple addition and subtraction of days, we need a handful of system functions to deal with dates and times. These functions are:

- DateAdd(datepart, number, date)
  DateAdd adds a number of days, months etc. to a given date.
  example:
  DateAdd(dd, 2, '2010-12-01')
  returns the date '2010-12-03'

- DateDiff(datepart, date1, date2)
  DateDiff returns the number of days, months etc. elapsed between date1 and date2
  example:
  DateDiff(dd, '2010-12-01', '1020-12-03')
  returns '3'

- DateName(datepart, date)
  Returns a string value for the specified part of a date
  example:
  DateName(mm, '2010-10-31')
  returns 'October'

- Day(date)
  Returns an integer value for the day part of a given date
  example:
  Day('2010-10-31')
  returns '31'

- Month(date)
  Returns an integer value for the month part of a given date
  example:
  Month('2010-10-31')
  returns '10'

- Year(date)
  Returns an integer value for the year part of a given date
  example:
  Year('2010-10-31')
  returns '2010'

- DatePart(datepart, date)
  Returns part of a date as an integer value
  example:
  DatePart(dd, '2010-10-31')
  returns '31'

The above examples almost all require an input that I've called 'datepart' which is a specific word or abbreviation indicating the part of the datetime object to which we are referring. Here is a partial list of common dateparts and their abbreviations:

- Year: yy, yyyy

- Quarter: q, qq

- Month: m, mm

- Day: d, dd

- Week: wk, ww

- Hour: h, hh

- Minute: n, mi

- Second: s, ss

For the most part, you'll want to use these just for simple comparative math. Using any of these functions inside of a SELECT query is likely to immediately turn your nice efficient seek into a nice slow scan. For example, while these two queries are logically identical:

```
SELECT * FROM History
WHERE timestamp > '2010-10-31 00:00:01'
AND timestamp < '2010-10-31 23:59:59'
```

```
-- is identical to
SELECT * FROM History
WHERE DateDiff(dd, timestamp, '2010-10-
31') = 0
```

The query using DateDiff even *looks* simpler, but be forewarned that the second query will result in an index or table scan while the first will allow for an index seek. On sufficiently small tables this is not necessarily a problem – the difference between a 10 millisecond execute time and a 20 millisecond execute time is trivial, of course. But imagine the difference on a historical data table with 20 million rows... Sadly this is something that I do not *have* to imagine...

Section 6.8: String Functions

String manipulation is also an integral part of many programming jobs and, as such, TSQL has a set of commands for string manipulation as well. These tend to be a bit more involved than some of the datetime functions and while datetime functions are no less important, string manipulation tends to happen more often. Here are the most commonly used string manipulation functions in TSQL:

- ASCII
  Returns the ASCII value of a given char
  example:
  ASCII('A'
  returns 65

- CHAR
  The reverse of the ASCII function, returns the character corresponding to a number
  example:
  CHAR(65)
  returns A

- CHARINDEX
  Returns the starting point of the first occurrence of one string within another string
  example:
  CHARINDEX('C', 'ABCDEFG')
  returns 3

- DIFFERENCE
  Returns a value between 0 and 4 reflecting how close a match there is between two strings, phonetically speaking; 0 being nowhere near a match, 4 being a perfect match.
  example:
  DIFFERENCE('Joe', 'Joseph')
  Returns 3

- LEFT
  Returns the leftmost characters from a string
  example:
  LEFT('Jill Smith', 4)
  returns 'Jill'

- LEN
  Returns the length of a string
  example:
  LEN('example')
  returns 7

- LOWER
  Returns the all-lowercase equivalent of a given string
  example:
  LOWER('David Perry')
  returns 'david perry'

- LTRIM
  Trims spaces and null characters from the left side of a string
  example:

LTRIM('   test   ')
returns 'test   '

- Nchar
  NChar is the Unicode equivalent to the CHAR function. It
  accepts an integer between 0 and 65,535 and returns a
  data type of nchar(1) with the corresponding Unicode
  character
  example: Nchar(931)
  returns 'Σ' (Greek Capital Sigma)

- PATINDEX
  Searches for patterns within a string. Similar to
  CHARINDEX except that it allows for wildcards
  example: PATINDEX('%jo%', 'james, john, jim')
  returns 8

- REPLACE
  Replaces all occurrences of one string within another
  string by a third string
  example: REPLACE('ababab', 'a', 'A')
  returns 'AbAbAb'

- REPLICATE
  Repeats a string expression a number of times
  example: REPLICATE('A', 10)
  returns 'AAAAAAAAAA'

- REVERSE
  Reverses the order of letters in a string
  example: REVERSE('abcd')
  returns 'dcba'

- Right
  Returns the rightmost characters of a string
  example: RIGHT('David Perry', 5)
  returns 'Perry'

- RTRIM
  Trims trailing spaces and null characters from the right side of a string
  example: RTRIM('   test   ')
  returns '   test'

- SPACE
  SPACE is a special-case version of REPLICATE that only creates spaces
  example: 'test' + SPACE(5) + 'test'
  returns 'test   test'

- STR
  Converts a numeric value to a string. This is largely deprecated since statements like 10 + '%' will usually result in implicit conversion to a string, but I still include it because explicit conversion is still occasionally necessary
  example: STR(123)
  returns '123' (note the quotes, this is a string now, so '2' + '2' = '22' and so on)

- STUFF
  Replaces a portion of one string with another. Syntax is STUFF(original_string, start, length, strint_to_insert)
  example: STUFF('David Perry', 5, 6, 'James')
  returns 'DaviJamesy'

- SUBSTRING
  Retrieves a part of a string, beginning at point x and returning y characters
  example: SUBSTRING('ABCDEFG', 3, 2)
  returns 'CD'

- UNICODE
  Returns the integer Unicode value of a char(1) or of the leftmost character in a string
  example: UNICODE('j')
  returns 106

- UPPER
  Converts a string to its all-uppercase equivalent
  example: UPPER('David Perry')
  returns 'DAVID PERRY'

Those of you with some previous programming background might notice that there is no SPLIT() function in TSQL. I can't speak to the reasons for such a blaring omission but there are a handful of ways around this. One simple method is to grievously misuse PARSENAME which is intended to return portions of DBO specifiers. PARSENAME('database1.dbo.table1', 3) for example, returns 'database1' (it reads right to left, so item 3 means 'third from the right' – item 1 would be 'table1'). If we wanted to split on spaces for example, we could do something like PARSENAME(REPLACE('David James Perry', ' ', '.'), 3) to replace all the spaces with dots. The above example would turn the string 'David James Perry' into 'David.James.Perry' and subsequently PARSENAME would return 'David' as the third object in the chain. Obviously this is a sub-optimal solution. Claytong of codeproject.com has written a stored procedure that performs a proper split and returns results as a table variable. It is 103 lines long so I will not publish it here in its entirety, but it can be found at:

http://www.codeproject.com/KB/database/SQL_UDF_to_Parse_a_String.aspx

Another common task we might want to perform that TSQL does not have a built-in function for is counting the number of occurrences of a substring – how often does the letter 'o' occur in 'John Doe' for example. Here's some complex looking code that's really pretty simple once we break it down:

```
DECLARE @start_len int
DECLARE @end_len int
DECLARE @start_string varchar(30)
DECLARE @sub_string varchar(30)
DECLARE @num_occur int
```

```
SET @start_len = LEN(@start_string)
set @start_string =
REPLACE(@start_string,
    @sub_string, '')
set @end_len = LEN(@start_string)
set @num_occur = @start_len - @end_len
set @num_occur = @num_occur /
LEN(@sub_string)
```

In the above code we've calculated the length of the starting string before we do anything to it, then replaced all occurrences of our desired substring . Now we calculate the length again, then subtract one from the other – the difference, of course, is the number of characters we removed. Divide that by the length of the substring itself and we've got the number of occurrences. This can be done in one single (albeit heavily nested) statement and without variables, but I've expanded it here for the purpose of clarity.

Section 6.9: Data Conversion Functions

There are only a handful of data conversion functions and, for the most part, SQL will implicitly handle conversions for you. Still, for those few occasions where explicit conversion is necessary it's important to know how to handle it. There are also a small handful of other functions that fall under the logical heading of "Data Conversion" that are used often enough to merit a mention.

- CAST
  Cast is a simple method for converting one data type to another. It is the ANSI standard for conversion but does not support any kind of formatting. Casting a datetime to varchar, for example, will always yield something like 'Jan 1 2010 1:24PM' and holds no option to format otherwise.
  example:

```
declare @d datetime
set @d = '2010-01-01 13:24:00'
SELECT CAST(@d as varchar(30))
```
returns: 'Jan 1 2010 1:24 PM'

- **COALESCE**

  Coalesce is a simplified version of a CASE expression that returns the first expression in a list which is not null. This is often used to default to zero if a variable is null or similar logic

  example: COALESCE(@variable, 0)

  returns: the value of @variable when said value is not null, or the value 0 when @variable contains a null value

- **CONVERT**

  Convert is similar to CAST except that it supports formatting for specific conversion types. It takes three arguments, separated by commas while CAST takes two, separated by the 'AS' keyword.

  example:

  ```
  declare @d datetime
  set @d = '2011-01-01 13:24:00'
  SELECT CONVERT(varchar(30), @d, 1)
  ```

  returns: '01/01/11'

  The third value is a format specifier as mentioned earlier. These specifiers are too numerous to be mentioned here, even briefly, but can be found at the following MSDN article:

  http://msdn.microsoft.com/en-us/library/aa226054

- **ISNULL**

  ISNULL is similar to COALESCE in that it replaces a null value with something else. The primary difference is that COALESCE will take an indeterminate number of arguments, selecting the first item in those arguments which is not null. ISNULL takes only two arguments, an expression which may or may not contain a null value, and the value to replace it with, should it be found to contain a null value.

  example: ISNULL(@d, 200)

78

returns: The value of @d if @d is not null, or 200 if @d is null

- NULLIF
  Returns a NULL value when two expressions are equal. If the two expressions are not equal, returns the first argument passed.
  example: NULLIF (@x, @y)
  returns: if @x is equal to @y, it will return NULL. Otherwise it will return @x

Section 6.10: Looping

In addition to flow control and math, one of the requisite components of any complete programming language, TSQL included, is the ability to construct a loop. A classic beginner's mistake in TSQL is to attempt (in my case for over an hour) to write a FOR/NEXT loop. TSQL's syntax is so similar to BASIC as to easily suggest that this should be the default looping structure, and FOR is even a real keyword in TSQL (it highlights blue in Query Analyzer/Management Studio) – turns out FOR is keyword to tell SQL how you would like your output formatted or specify the SELECT statement for a cursor.

As it turns out, the default looping structure in SQL is the WHILE loop. Its syntax is as follows:

```
WHILE expression
  {statement|BEGIN...END}
  [BREAK]
  [CONTINUE]
```

A loop designed to print 'Hello World' five times, for example, would look like this:

```
DECLARE @i int
SET @i = 0
WHILE @i < 5
BEGIN
  PRINT 'Hello World'
  SET @i = @i + 1
END
```

While loops do not have to execute a given number of times – they can also be made to continue or end based upon specific logic. If, for example, we have a process that needs to be delayed until another process finishes and we have no idea how long that will take, we could have the first process write to a table when it finishes and then put something like this at the beginning of the second:

```
DECLARE @done_flag int
SELECT @done_flag = proc_done FROM
proc_status
WHILE @done_flag = 0
BEGIN
  WAITFOR DELAY '00:01:00'
  SELECT @done_flag = proc_done from
proc_status
END
-- Other code goes here
```

The above code will check once per minute to see if the proc_done flag in the proc_status table has changed. When it is no longer equal to zero, the loop will be broken and the code below the loop will begin execution. We can also manually control the flow of the loop from within using the CONTINUE and BREAK commands. Here's another way we could have written the above code:

```
WHILE 1=1
BEGIN
  IF SELECT proc_done FROM proc_status =
0
  BEGIN
    WAITFOR DELAY '00:01:00'
    CONTINUE
  END
  ELSE
    BREAK
END
```

The WHILE statement requires an expression, but that doesn't mean we can't give it an expression that will always resolve as true. By asking WHILE to loop so long as one equals one, we can trick it into creating an infinite loop. Within the loop, we have a standard IF/ELSE based on the result of the same SELECT we did in the last example, but we've also used the new keywords CONTINUE and BREAK. CONTINUE tells SQL to skip the rest of what's in the WHILE loop and jump back up to the top. BREAK tells the WHILE loop to end whether its conditions have been met or not.

Now that we know a thing or two about loops, let's talk about the most useful thing we can do with them...

Section 6.11: Cursors & Dynamic SQL

Cursors give us a method for looping through a recordset and performing actions on/with each record. Here is an example of a functioning cursor, we'll talk about its constituent parts in a moment:

```
DECLARE @name varchar(50)
DECLARE db_cursor CURSOR FOR
  SELECT name FROM
MASTER.dbo.sysdatabases
  WHERE name NOT IN ('master', 'model',
    'msdb', 'tempdb')
OPEN db_cursor
FETCH NEXT FROM db_cursor INTO @name
WHILE @@FETCH_STATUS = 0
BEGIN
  DBCC CHECKDB(@name, REPAIR_FAST)
  FETCH NEXT FROM db_cursor INTO @name
END
CLOSE db_cursor
DEALLOCATE db_cursor
```

The above code is probably the longest and most complex example in the book thus far. First we declare a variable of a type cursor, but we must specify what it is a cursor FOR. In this case we've created a SELECT statement that should return the names of each non-system database on the current server. Next we tell SQL to open the cursor – this is the point at which it actually performs our SELECT. The FETCH NEXT statement tells SQL to grab the next row from a given cursor and store its value in a variable. Cursors handle their own self-incrementing counters and cannot read in reverse, so be sure to do everything you need with a given cursor row while you've got it – as soon as you FETCH again, there's no going back. Our WHILE loop checks the @@FETCH_STATUS system variable to see if we've still got records left or if we've reached the end of the recordset. We've got a DBCC CHECKDB with the REPAIR_FAST option inside the loop, so the purpose of this script is obviously to perform repairs on all databases, and then finally after we finish our loop we close and deallocate the cursor.

Closing the cursor is obvious enough, after all we opened it up at the top, right? Close just does the opposite, closes the connection the cursor was populated from. Deallocate, on the other hand, is new. Most variables are automatically deallocated at the end of execution, and cursors are no exception. SQL has its own garbage collection routines and they work quite well, so why explicitly deallocate the cursor? Well, unlike a simple integer or varchar, a cursor holds the entire recordset produced by its accompanying SQL statement, which can be quite large and take up a lot of memory. We explicitly deallocate cursors because it's good practice to make 100% sure that large memory-hungry constructs are disposed of. Also, in a complex process involving many cursors, each one not disposed of adds up until the process is completely finished – garbage collection only occurs at the end of the batch – this can create horribly inefficient processes that will bog down your server every time they execute.

Another powerful concept that often goes hand in hand with cursors is dynamic SQL. Dynamic SQL, in its most basic form, gives you the ability to store a SQL query in a string and execute that SQL statement. This means that you can dynamically build a SQL statement at the time of execution and then run it. Here's an example:

```
DECLARE @vSQL varchar(50)
SET @vSQL = 'DROP TABLE table1'
EXEC(@vSQL)
```

The above code stores a SQL statement in a varchar variable and then EXECs that varchar variable. This example is a bit nonsensical since we could just as easily have replaced the whole mess with the DROP statement itself, but it should be easy enough to see how we could use various bits of branching logic, string manipulation, etc. to dynamically build and execute SQL statements in a meaningful way.

Section 6.12: Error Handling

One thing common to all programming languages is that errors happen. If you're anything like me, most of these will be typos. Still, it's good to know how to check for errors and handle them. One thing that can make your life much easier is setting the XACT_ABORT server variable for your batches.

With XACT_ABORT set to ON, most errors will abort the batch and attempt to roll back as best as possible. Keep in mind, however, that XACT_ABORT does not affect compilation errors, such as those encountered in EXEC statements or dynamic SQL, so any time you use EXEC you should be prepared to do some basic error handling.

Basic error handling in SQL looks something like this:

```
-- Do something that might raise an
error
IF @@error <> 0
-- Do your error handling
```

The system variable @@error holds the last error code thrown by the current batch. As long as that error code is zero, then no errors have occurred. Your error handling will, of course, depend upon what you were doing when the error occurred. If you were declaring a cursor, for example, you'd want to deallocate it in your error handling branch. If you were doing something inside of a loop, you could BREAK out of the loop, etc.

What if we want to do the exact opposite of handle an error – what if we want to react to some bit of logic by creating an error? The necessity to do so arises quite often, to ensure that valid values are passed to your stored procedures, for example. In such a case we could use the RAISERROR command, like so:

```
RAISERROR ('Invalid Value', 16, 1)
```

The above statement will throw an error with severity 18, state 1 and error text of 'Invalid Value' – These values can be found using the system procedures ERROR_MESSAGE(), ERROR_SEVERITY(), and ERROR_STATE() respectively. The severity field indicates how bad the error might be, with higher numbers being worse than lower ones. Most of the errors you'll be manually throwing will be severity 0 to 10, which are informational messages only and will not cause most applications to display an error and end execution. Any severity above 10 will cause the database connection to be terminated, and user-generated errors in this range usually stop at severity 16. Depending on the alerts configured, an error of severity 17 or higher may trigger drastic actions or at the very least, wake the DBA up in the middle of the night.

A more advanced form of error handling than the simple 'IF @@error' block is the TRY/CATCH block familiar to many developers. The Try/Catch block will catch execution errors with a severity higher than 10 and, if possible, stop them from closing the database connection. Here is an example of TRY/CATCH:

```
BEGIN TRY
  -- Do something stupid
  -- Like divide by zero
  SELECT 1/0
END TRY
BEGIN CATCH
  -- Handle the error
END CATCH
```

In the above example we intentionally divide by zero to throw an error. The contents of the CATCH block can be anything from using different logic now that we know the denominator of our problem is zero or simply throwing a different error customized to the reasons why we might be dividing by zero.

Keep in mind that no amount of error handling will allow a snippet of code to execute which has compile errors. For example:

```
SELCT * FRM table1 WHER fld1=@var
```

This will never execute, no matter how you set XACT ABORT or whether you put it in a TRY/CATCH block. SQL will stop this code before it can even be evaluated to throw an error because it contains syntax errors or unrecognized commands.

Section 6.13: System Functions

There are a great many system functions in SQL server, of varying degrees of usefulness. While the subset of these you're likely to use varies greatly by task, here's a short list of the ones you're most likely to need.

- **APP_NAME**
  Returns the name of the application executing the query
  example: SELECT APP_NAME()
  returns: 'Microsoft SQL Server Management Studio –
  Query'

- **DecryptByPassphrase**
  In its simplest form, this takes two inputs – a value to
  encrypt and a password.
  example: DecryptByPassphrase('password',
  @text_to_decrypt)
  returns: decrypted text.
  This function can also take two more fields, indicating
  whether an authenticator was encrypted along with the
  plaintext. The authenticator is a checksum of the
  plaintext and an additional field which ensures that the
  data has not been changed. Such a statement might
  look like this:
  example: DecryptByPassphrase('password',
  @text_to_decrypt, 1, @authenticator)
  Where the 1 indicates that there is, in fact, an
  authenticator and @authenticator holds the value the
  text was encrypted with.

- **EncryptByPassphrase**
  EncryptByPassphrase is the logical opposite of
  DecryptByPassphrase and takes the same basic
  arguments except than instead of taking encrypted
  varBinary data and spitting out a string, it takes a string
  as input and returns varBinary data.
  example: EncryptByPassphrase('password,
  @text_to_encrypt)

- **DecryptByAsymKey**
  The great limitation of EncryptByPassPhrase is that it
  always performs triple-DES encryption, the security of
  which is almost completely dependent upon the quality
  of the passphrase used, which is not subjected to
  minimum complexity standards. DecryptByAsymKey

allows us to create an asymmetrical key of any type supported by the system and use it to encrypt and decrypt data. This is too complex to highlight within the context of this list, so a full code demo will be available at the end of this list.

- **EncryptByAsymKey**
  See: DecryptByAsymKey

- **Xp_cmdshell**
  Simultaneously the most powerful and scariest command available on most servers. This command is typically restricted to the server admin user/group only, and for good reason. The xp_cmdshell command takes one input, a string, and executes that input as a DOS command on the server. The command executes under the same account the SQL service is running under and inherits whatever permissions that account has. This procedure resides in the master database, and depending on your settings may need to be referenced as such. In newer versions this is disabled by default but can be re-enabled via sp_configure.
  example: exec master.dbo.xp_cmdshell 'dir c:'
  returns: directory listing of c:\

- **Sp_configure**
  Allows configuration of SQL server options. Simply running 'EXEC sp_configure' will list the config options that can be set. Sp_configure can also be called with the name of an option and a value and the keyword RECONFIGURE to change the value. Sp_configure changes server-wide options.
  example:
  EXEC sp_configure 'max server memory', 250
  RECONFIGURE
  GO

- **Sp_dboption**
  sp_dboption is similar to sp_configure except that it

holds database-specific settings. Its usage and syntax is the same, except that it does not require a RECONFIGURE

- **Sp_help**
  Provides information about a database object. Executed with no arguments, it returns a list of database objects accessible from the current context. Executed with one argument (a database object, by name) it returns information about the named object. Unlike sp_configure or sp_dboption, sp_help is read-only

- **Sp_recompile**
  sp_recompile forces a specified stored procedure or the triggers on a specified table to recompile the next time the table/procedure is accessed
  example: sp_recompile procedure_name

- **Sp_monitor**
  Monitors the performance of your server.

Asymmetric Key En/Decryption Example:

```
-- First we need to create a key
CREATE ASYMMETRIC KEY Key1
WITH Algorithm = RSA_1024
GO
-- Now let's use it
DECLARE @secret varchar(255) =
'cleartext phrase'
DECLARE @encrypted varbinary(max)
SET @encrypted =
ENCRYPTBYASYMKEY(ASYMKEY_ID(Key1),secret
)
SELECT @encrypted
SELECT
DECRYPTBYASYMKEY(ASYMKEY_ID(Key1),@encry
pted)
```

The above code creates a 1024-bit encryption key using the RSA algorithm and then uses it to encrypt the text stored in the @secret variable. We then use the same key to decrypt the same data. It should be noted that encrypted data should be stored in a varbinary field whenever possible. Allowing implicit or explicit conversion to other data types is not only wasteful of storage space but also allows for accidental corruption of data during the conversion process (ex: did I use varchar or nvarchar for this?).

Section 6.14: System Settings

Similar to system functions, there are a lot of system settings which you may use from time to time, but their usefulness will be entirely determined by your specific purposes. Again I'll present a short list of the most common candidates.

- HOST_NAME()
  Returns the host name (computer name) of the currently logged in user/session

- OBJECT_ID()
  Takes a string as an input and returns the numeric ID associated with the database object specified in the string, assuming one exists.

- OBJECT_NAME()
  Takes an integer as an input and returns the name of the database object with that ID, if one exists.

- SUSER_NAME()
  Returns the username of the current session. This will either return a windows domain account or a SQL account, depending on what authentication method is/are enabled and in use.

Chapter 7: Crystal Reports

Crystal Reports is a framework for creating reports using SQL as a data source. It is also possible to integrate such reports into your applications, but that is beyond the scope of this book. I'll be using Crystal Reports version 9, as that is the version I most commonly see in the corporate environment, but if your version is a little different, don't worry too much, they all look and work roughly the same.

Section 7.1: Creating Reports

When you first launch crystal reports, you'll be greeted by a dialog box something like this:

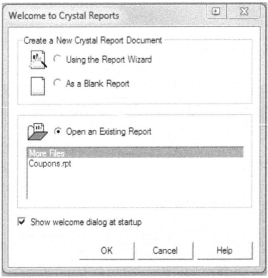

Figure 7.1: Crystal Reports Starting Dialog

This is foreshadowing of things to come: this dialog is standard and simple, just like everything else we're about to see. For now let's start with a blank report. You'll be prompted to select the connection to your database, if one does not exist create a new connection and use OLE DB for MS SQL. Next select the table you'll be querying for your report and move them to the right-hand list. If you'll be joining more than one table together, you can go to the "Links" tab and drag the linked fields from one table to another.

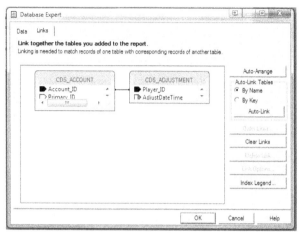

Figure 7.2: Links Dialog

When you've finished setting up your connections, tables and links, click OK to begin designing your report.

If you've ever written a report in Microsoft Access before, this should look very familiar – the interface is almost identical. You're probably looking at something like this:

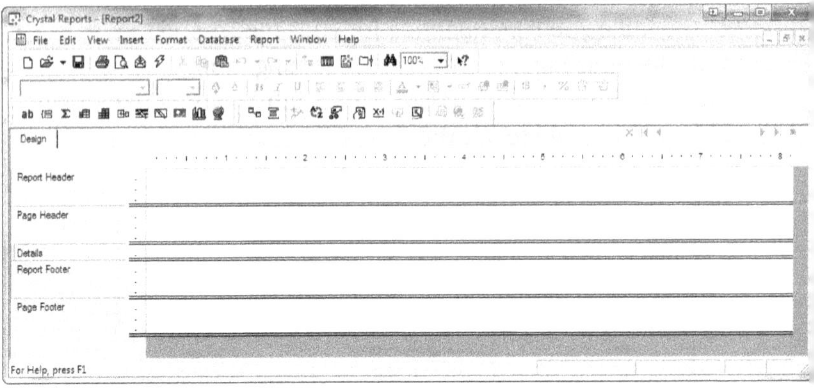
Crystal Reports - [Report2]
File Edit View Insert Format Database Report Window Help
Design
Report Header
Page Header
Details
Report Footer
Page Footer
For Help, press F1

Figure 7.3: Crystal Reports Design View

Go to your "View" menu and select "Field Explorer" – you should see something like this appear at the left side of your screen:

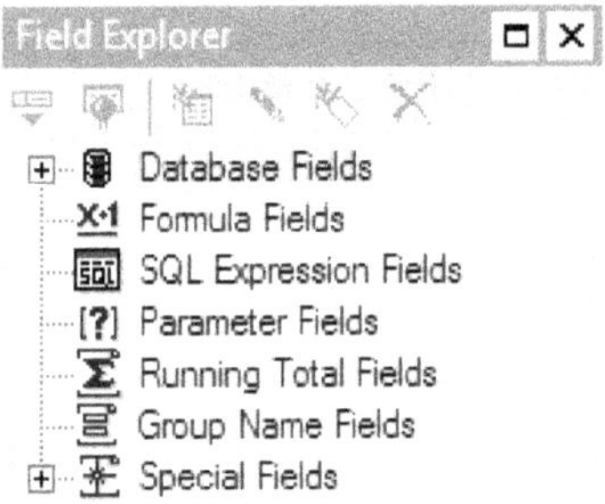
Field Explorer
Database Fields
Formula Fields
SQL Expression Fields
Parameter Fields
Running Total Fields
Group Name Fields
Special Fields

Figure 7.4: Field Explorer

The "Database Fields" item at the top of the list should expand to show all tables you entered in the previous dialog as well as their respective fields. To add a field to your report, simply drag it from the Field Explorer dialog to the Details area of your report. Items in the Details area will be reproduced once for each record found when the report runs.

There are also a number of Special Fields under the menu of the same name which may be useful for headers and footers including the date and time the report was run, the page number, page counts, record counts and so on. Labels may be added by clicking on the "Insert Text Object" button on your toolbar (**ab**) and placing the label with your mouse.

You can also include summary fields by clicking on your Insert menu then Summary, or by clicking on the "Summary" button on your toolbar (Σ). Select the desired field from the dropdown box at the top, then select the kind of summary you'd like. If these summary options look familiar, it's because we went over them in the previous chapter on queries.

Now that you've got a few things on your page, you might want to see what your report is going to look like. To generate a preview, click on the Preview button on your toolbar ( ). This will create (if it doesn't already exist) and switch to the Preview Tab. To return to designing your report, select the Design tab again.

Sometimes you will want to group your information by a field, just like in SQL. To accomplish this, click on the Group button on your toolbar ( ) and select the field to group by, as well as the sort order. It will add a new section of headers and footers surrounding the Details section of your report.

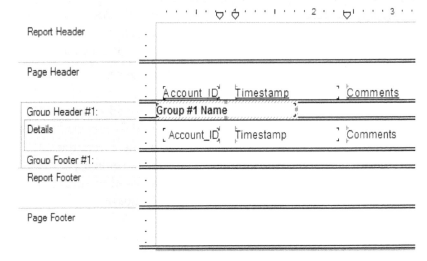

Figure 7.5: Group Header and Footer

All the records for a given grouping will appear in their own details section between a header and footer that distinguish each group. If you would only like to show the group information, without showing the details, you can suppress the display of the details section by right-clicking on the section's label and selecting "Suppress (No Drill-Down)" from the context menu.

Section 7.2: Using the SELECT Expert

So far we've been creating reports with no criteria – that is, reports based on a SELECT statement with no WHERE clause. Most of the time we're going to need to filter our data in order for it to be useful. This is where the Select Expert comes in.

To access the Select Expert, click on the "Select Expert" button on your toolbar (🐞). You should be presented with the following dialog:

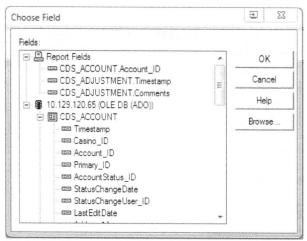

Figure 7.6: Select Expert Dialog 1

Select the field you will be filtering based on and click OK. You will now be presented with another simple dialog:

Figure 7.7: Select Expert Dialog 2

From the dropdown list, select whatever comparison is most appropriate to your filtering desires and select appropriate options for whatever new dropdowns or text boxes appear. Alternately, clicking "Show Formula" will present a text box at the bottom of the dialog with options surprisingly similar to what we already know from SQL. For my report I've opted to click on "Formula Editor" and change my comparison to run against the last 30 days. You can select the various functions and operators appropriate to your report from the list or, eventually, you'll have a fair set memorized and can simply type them in

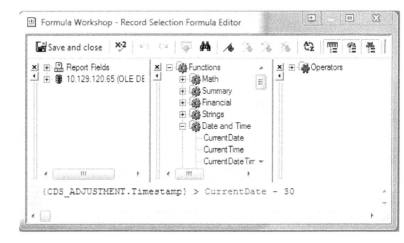

Figure 7.8: Formula Editor

The Select Expert allows for all of the standard SQL comparison operators (less than, greater than, equal to, in, between and so on) which should not be surprising since it is simply crafting a SQL statement from your various entries and executing it.

One more powerful option in Crystal Reports is "Parameter Fields." Parameter Fields are stand-ins for data that may not be known until it is time to run the report. A user might want to look for records with a timestamp between two dates, or a dollar amount within a certain range. We might not know what these ranges are until the report is actually run.

To add a parameter field, right click on "Parameter Fields" in Field Explorer and select "New." You should be presented with the following dialog:

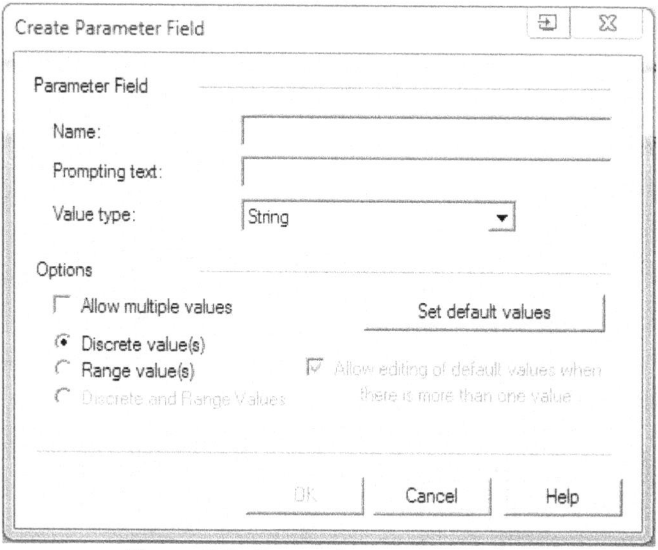

Figure 7.9: Create Parameter Dialog

Just like SQL variables, parameters have names and types. They also have "Prompting Text" that indicates to the user what information they are attempting to enter. I've added two parameters to my report: StartDate and EndDate. Now let's go back to our Select Expert and see how we use those Parameter fields.

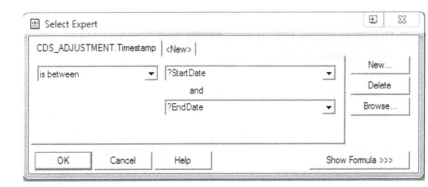

Figure 7.10: Using Parameter Fields

Just like we specify variables in SQL using the @ sign, we signify them in Crystal Reports using a question mark. Here I've specified that I want only records timestamped between the user-provided start and end times. Note that Parameter Fields not used in any filters will not be prompted for – if nothing is done with the data, the user will not be asked to provide it.

Now if we try to preview our report, we'll be prompted to enter our parameters.

Figure 7.11: Parameter Values Prompt

To change the sorting of your report, click on the "Report" menu and select either "Record Sort Expert" or "Group Sort Expert" as appropriate. Move the field(s) to sort on to the list at the right and select the appropriate sort order.

Using the same methods we've already used to build formulas and SQL expressions elsewhere in SQL, we can insert Formula and SQL Expression fields by right-clicking on the appropriate root item in Field Explorer and selecting "New." Once again, we can use language almost identical to SQL to create fields for our report that are mathematically calculated or logically decided. Crystal Reports contains over 300 pre-written functions, so to even attempt a listing here would be madness. The full functionality of Crystal Reports deserves its own book, but thankfully you won't likely need anywhere near that much knowledge to be functional.

Right-clicking on any item in your report should give you the option to format that item. All standard formatting abilities are within these dialogs including font, style, size, color and so on. Many of the formatting options in these dialogs will have a Conditional Formatting button () next to them. Clicking one of these buttons will allow you to set conditional formatting for that field. If, for example, you wanted to format negative numbers in red then you might enter a formula like:

```
IF {Amount} < 0 THEN crRed ELSE crBlack
```

In the conditional formatting block for the color field. The appropriate color constants can be found in the Functions box at the top center of the conditional formatting dialog.

There is so much more to Crystal Reports than what we've covered here, but this very basic overview as well as some simple experimentation should serve you well for all but the most complex of reports.

Chapter 8: MySQL

MySQL is a relational database management system similar in many ways to Microsoft's SQL implementation. Since there are some distinct similarities, we won't spend a lot of time on these specifics. Instead we'll talk about the biggest differences between the two platforms.

The first thing you might notice about MySQL is that there really isn't a set front-end for it like there is with Microsoft's SQL product. There are at least a dozen different applications to administer your databases and run queries. Probably the most popular are MySQL Workbench, SQLYog, HeidiSQL and phpMyAdmin, depending on your platform and requirements. Of these, SQLYog is probably the most like the Microsoft environment and while it is a commercial product, there is a free "Community Edition" available for download.

While Microsoft maintains a hefty majority share for desktop applications and intranet-based solutions, MySQL is the database platform of choice for web applications and has become ubiquitous since the advent of LAMP (Linux, Apache, MySQL, PHP) servers as a simple pre-installable choice for many Linux distributions. MySQL powers many of the most popular and well-known sites on the internet including Flickr, Youtube, Wikipedia, Google and Facebook. It's a perfectly capable database engine once you get used to a few minor differences.

First, the types of JOINs available varies slightly. Both support the standard keywords discussed earlier, but Microsoft's solution lacks support for Natural joins and the "Using" clause. Natural joins are a special-case join in which identically named columns containing identical data in both tables are merged, rather than producing a separate column for each table's copy of the data. The Using clause is simply a shorter method for specifying the columns to join on. Consider the following:

```
SELECT * FROM transactions
LEFT JOIN employees
USING (teller_id, employee_id)
```

The above query is logically identical to this query, using Microsoft's required, expanded nomenclature:

```
SELECT * FROM transactions
LEFT JOIN employees
ON transactions.teller_id =
employees.employee_id
AND employees.employee_id =
transactions.teller_id
```

The "Using" keyword indicates a bidirectional equality without having to specify quite so many names and relationships. Just the first of many ways that MySQL differs subtly from the Microsoft solution.

For limiting result sets, neither Microsoft nor MySQL follow the ANSI-92 standard. Here is the same query written in ANSI-92, Microsoft and MySQL nomenclature:

```
-- ANSI-92 Standard
SELECT * FROM table1
FETCH FIRST 1 ROWS ONLY

-- Microsoft SQL
SELECT TOP 1 * FROM table1

-- MySQL
SELECT * FROM table1 LIMIT 1
```

103

Not much meaningful difference in total query length between the two, but both are certainly shorter than the ANSI standard, so I suppose I can understand the deviation.

MySQL and Microsoft SQL also differ in what data types they support. In older versions of Microsoft's SQL server, there was support for the ANSI standard BOOLEAN type, but newer versions have done away with it and replaced it with the "Bit" data type. MySQL offers a true Boolean type, but it is non-conforming in a rather interesting way. MySQL's Boolean data type is actually just an alias for a tinyint field, and the constants "true" and "false" are just aliases for 1 and 0 respectively. Because of this alias, one can counter-intuitively assign a value of 5 to a Boolean field without error. The tinyint data type also consumes much more storage space than the bit data type, though MySQL *does* offer a bit data type that can be used in much the same way as Microsoft's.

The ANSI standard also specifies a function called CHARACTER_LENGTH which is replaced in Microsoft's implementation with the LEN function. MySQL does not implement the function under the name LEN but rather under the ANSI specification name CHARACTER_LENGTH. Other than the name difference, the functionality is identical.

Like many other converts from Windows-based to Linux-based solutions, you may be shocked to realize that almost everything in the Linux world is case sensitive. This is the case with most of MySQL's string manipulation functions as well. REPLACE, for example is identical in both Microsoft and MySQL except that Microsoft breaks the ANSI standard by defaulting to case-insensitivity.

Another place where Microsoft breaks standard while MySQL holds firm is with the TRIM function. Microsoft offers non-standard trimming in the form of LTRIM() and RTRIM()

which trim leading spaces from the left and right sides respectively. The ANSI standard, as well as the MySQL implementation takes the following form:

```
TRIM(specifier FROM string)
```

Where "specifier" can be "LEADING," "TRAILING" or "BOTH" such that one statement retains the functionality of both LTRIM() and RTRIM() as well as their combined LTRIM(RTRIM()) functionality.

In Microsoft SQL I've become far too comfortable using + as the string concatenation operator. In fact, this is another example of both sides breaking the rules. The ANSI-92 standard for string concatenation is to use the || operator (double-pipe). Microsoft, of course, breaks this standard by using + and MySQL breaks this even worse by using || as a shortcut for the "OR" keyword. MySQL provides a function "CONCAT(string1, string2)" for string concatenation, which accepts two or more arguments. If any single argument passed to CONCAT is null, then the entire output will be null.

One of the rare areas where MS SQL follows the standard perfectly and MySQL does not is with IDENTITY fields. An IDENTITY field is an integer field that is assumed to be unique and automatically increments as new records are added. Microsoft follows the standard normally, while MySQL allows for the creation of a normal integer column with the standard UNIQUE constraint and a non-standard AUTO_INCREMENT attribute.

Other differences include getting a list of databases (MSSQL = "EXEC SP_HELPDB", MySQL = "SHOW DATABASES"), updating table statistics (MSSQL = "UPDATE STATISTICS", MySQL = "ANALYZE TABLE"), TCP/IP port (MSSQL=1433, MySQL=63306) and so on.

Aside from this handful of differences, Microsoft SQL Server and MySQL both seem to support the same basic structures. There is little difference in implementation of WHERE loops, IF/ELSE IF/ELSE branching structures, BEGIN and END blocks etc. A handful of built-in procedures are available in MySQL that are not available in Microsoft SQL, just as there are some built-ins available to Microsoft SQL users that will not be available to MySQL, but the basic functionality tends to be cross-platform.

In the end, both server platforms are quite capable and should serve well enough for most small to medium business needs without modification. There are, of course, other solutions available (PostgreSQL, Oracle, DB2, Informix etc.) but that's a story for another book.

Conclusions and Credits

The more dependent upon information technology our society becomes, the more data we will generate and the more databases we will require. We are already reaching a point where current database technologies cannot handle the amounts of data we are capable of generating without significant modification. What will the databases of tomorrow look like? Will the two-dimensional tables of old still be sufficient or will we be working with 3, 4, or 5 dimensional data sets? What kind of visual structures could we even use to present such a recordset? These questions are, so far, unanswered – but one thing is absolutely certain: There has never been a better time in human history to be in the business of data management.

* * * * *

Thanks For Reading!

www.ingramcontent.com/pod-product-compliance
Lightning Source LLC
Chambersburg PA
CBHW052148070326
40689CB00050B/2511